A NEW BODY–MIND APPROACH

A NEW BODY–MIND APPROACH
Clinical Cases

Jean Benjamin Stora

Translated by Sophie Leighton

LONDON AND NEW YORK

First published in French as *La Nouvelle Approche Psychosomatique: 9 Cas Cliniques*
© MJW Fédition
First published 2015 by Karnac Books Ltd.

Published 2018 by Routledge
2 Park Square, Milton Park, Abingdon, Oxon OX14 4RN
711 Third Avenue, New York, NY 10017, USA

Routledge is an imprint of the Taylor & Francis Group, an informa business

Copyright for this English translation © 2015 Sophie Leighton

The right of Jean Benjamin Stora to be identified as the author of this work has been asserted in accordance with §§ 77 and 78 of the Copyright Design and Patents Act 1988.

All rights reserved. No part of this book may be reprinted or reproduced or utilised in any form or by any electronic, mechanical, or other means, now known or hereafter invented, including photocopying and recording, or in any information storage or retrieval system, without permission in writing from the publishers.

Notice:
Product or corporate names may be trademarks or registered trademarks, and are used only for identification and explanation without intent to infringe.

British Library Cataloguing in Publication Data

A C.I.P. for this book is available from the British Library

ISBN-13: 9781782200987 (pbk)

Typeset by V Publishing Solutions Pvt Ltd., Chennai, India

CONTENTS

ACKNOWLEDGEMENTS	vii
ABOUT THE AUTHOR	ix
PREFACE	xi
FOREWORD by Mark Solms	xiii
FOREWORD	xv
INTRODUCTION	xxxiii
CHAPTER ONE Marie-Laure and metabolic syndrome: relations between the psychic apparatus and the hypothalamic axis	1
CHAPTER TWO Chloé: repairing the psychic apparatus—neuronal tumour, neuropsychoanalysis, or neuropsychosomatics?	21

CHAPTER THREE
Claude: "The Little Prince's heartache"   49

CHAPTER FOUR
A hypochondriac patient—the enigma of Damien's
    somatic problems   61

CHAPTER FIVE
Lucien: type 2 diabetic; the patient's cultural dimension,
    denial of illness and narcissistic problematic   85

CHAPTER SIX
Alicia: "when I've had the transplant, will I feel better?"   109

CHAPTER SEVEN
The heart problems of a "famous patient"   123

CHAPTER EIGHT
Conclusion   135

NOTES   139

REFERENCES   145

INDEX   149

ACKNOWLEDGEMENTS

I would first like to express my gratitude to Prof. Mareike Wolf-Fédida, who encouraged me to write this book and accepted it for publication;

to Prof. Jean-François Allilaire, who since 1993 has followed and supported my clinical and therapeutic work in the departments at La Pitié-Salpêtrière;

to Prof. Marc-Olivier Bitker, who allowed me to conduct clinical examinations of patients in the kidney-pancreas transplant unit, and who helped me to set up the university diploma in integrative psychosomatics with Jean-François Allilaire;

to Prof. Éric Bruckert, head of the endocrinology department, who provided space for the psychosomatics practice that is open to all the medical departments at La Pitié-Salpêtrière;

to Prof. Agnès Hartemann, head of the diabetology department, who allowed me to participate in the staff of the "struggling diabetologists", whose main objective is to improve patient care by reintegrating their psychic and family dimensions;

to Dr Philippe Giral, who is the doctor with whom I have had the most discussions over the last nineteen years;

To my friend and colleague, Jean-Michel Fourcade, Director of the Nouvelle Faculté Libre, who has supported my teaching and research in integrative psychosomatics.

To my earliest mentor, Dr Moïse Maïmonides (1135–1204), who, as the first psychosomatician, developed a general approach to patients and illnesses; his vast medical œuvre reveals him as a very fine clinician, and I have learnt a great deal from him. He was the doctor of Saladin, the first sultan of Egypt and Syria.

To Averroes, Abu'l-Walid Muhammad bin 'Ahmad bin Rušd (1126–1198), and to his master Avenzoar, Ibn Zuhr (رهز نبا), one of the great doctors of his era, who influenced European medicine up to the seventeenth century. Jewish and Arab medicine still share this characteristic of taking a psychosomatic approach to patients.

ABOUT THE AUTHOR

Jean Benjamin Stora is a psychoanalyst and psychosomatician, and a consultant in psychosomatics at La Pitié-Salpêtrière Hospital, Paris. In 2006, he established the university diploma in integrative psychosomatics, psychoanalysis, medicine, and the neurosciences, which he co-directs at the Faculté de Médecine, Université Pierre et Marie Curie, Paris 6. He was president of the Pierre Marty Institute of Psychosomatics from 1989 to 1992, and of the Société Française de Médecine Psychosomatique from 2000 to 2002. He is the author of many books, including *Le Stress, Quand le corps prend la relève, stress traumatismes et maladies somatiques, Vivre avec une greffe, accueillir l'autre, Neuropsychanalyse, Controverses et Dialogues, When the Body Displaces the Mind*, and *La nouvelle approche psychosomatique, cas cliniques*.

PREFACE

To my patients at La Pitié-Salpêtrière hospital, who by their trust have helped me enormously in developing integrative psychosomatics as a scientific and clinical field.

To all my colleagues, medical professors, hospital doctors, clinic directors, and specialist doctors, alongside whom I have worked over the past nineteen years, who have facilitated my investigations and helped me to gain a better understanding of their clinical practices in a highly technologised hospital—some of whom are making major efforts to reintroduce the dimension of the subject into their clinical approach. I would also like to thank the nurses in the metabolic syndrome unit, who have supported and encouraged my psychosomatic approach with patients throughout these years.

To all my students who have attended the integrative psychosomatics courses at the faculty of medicine, whose questions have enabled me to progress in explaining the concepts and the clinical practice. And to all my colleagues and members of the Société de psychosomatique intégrative. It goes without saying that there are still many questions that remain unanswered; but who, in the scientific domain, can answer every question?

Jean Benjamin Stora,
Paris
Revised for the English edition

FOREWORD

Jean Benjamin Stora is a clinician of vast experience. In his psychosomatics practice at La Pitié-Salpêtrière, he has personally examined over 3000 patients, with a wide range of illnesses, building on the work of his great teacher, Pierre Marty, while he developed the deeply integrative approach that he describes in this book. In a very real sense, therefore, the book we are now holding in our hands is the product of a lifetime's work. The yield of this work is an achievement second to none other: the integration into physical medicine of the mental apparatus—a "system" not fundamentally different from the other functional systems of the body, such as the digestive and respiratory systems.

Let us not forget: we *must* find an integrated place for the mental function alongside the other vital functions of the body. It is surely no accident that the mental function evolved. It is not an epiphenomenon—nice to have—it must actually do something of biological importance. The mindless body of a complex organism is accordingly not viable. It will die, just as surely as the comatose patient will die if not cared for by other minds.

Simply put, it is the role of the mental function to register the vital and reproductive needs of the organism and then to act upon them in such a way that they can be met, through interaction with the external object world, which is the only place where bodily needs can ever be met.

That is the task of the mental function. The complexity of the task is a measure of how difficult life is.

The registration of needs generates drives ("measures of the demand made upon the mind to perform work") which are felt as homeostatic affects, which in turn give rise to activation of instincts ("primal phantasies" in the nomenclature of Freud) with more complex object-related affects of their own. Even these basic mental capacities are sometimes compromised, before we can even speak of memory traces of perceptual representations and re-representations ("thing presentations" and "word presentations") and the cognitive gymnastics they give rise to. We learn in the pages of this book, from Stora's rich clinical descriptions, how catastrophic the consequences of such failures may be.

No neuroscientist can deny these facts. But it took psychoanalysts like Jean Benjamin Stora to trace the clinical implications for the life of the mind, sometimes surprising implications, in relation to actual individual cases; and this is a very great service to us all (whether we all realise it or not).

I cannot recommend this work too highly, to all my colleagues: psychoanalysts, physicians, and surgeons alike.

Mark Solms

FOREWORD

I met Pierre Marty in 1984, having completed a long psychoanalytic journey at the psychoanalytic institute of the Paris Psychoanalytical Society. I began to practise psychoanalysis in 1973 in parallel with my teaching career at a Grande École in France. From the age of fifteen, I wanted to treat somatic patients and to become a doctor like my maternal uncles, but a serious eye accident had prevented me from fulfilling this wish. After the doctors had stabilised my condition, and had advised me against undertaking lengthy studies such as medicine, I was able to pursue studies in law, economics, management, and psychology, but deep down my desire to heal was unaltered. The doctors had treated me, and enabled me to see without suspecting that my condition was going to stabilise over the long-term, they formed the hypothesis of blindness; in the process, my vocation had not disappeared.

Pierre Marty's analytically-inspired psychosomatics enabled me to fulfil a deep vocation, and for this I will always be grateful to him. At the end of my training, Pierre Marty suggested that I become the president of the institution that he had founded in 1972.[1] I carried out this mission until July 1992, when my term of office came to an end and also my teacher's serious illness emerged, from which he was to die in June 1993 at La Pitié-Salpêtrière. Following insistent demands from my former colleagues at this institution, I had to leave, and with the help of Professors Jean-François Allilaire and Marc-Olivier Bitker I established a psychosomatics practice at La Pitié-Salpêtrière hospital, which was based in the endocrinology department and also open to patients from every other department.

At the Institute of Psychosomatics, I had not been able to conduct clinical examinations without supervision; the teaching was traditional and we attended the clinical investigations of our teachers, who were "qualified psychosomaticians" (as I later became). La Pitié-Salpêtrière (with its medical professors and hospital doctors) has allowed me, over the last nineteen years, to conduct clinical examinations of over 3,000 patients suffering from various diseases. Thanks to this remarkable hospital experience, I was gradually able to develop a new psychosomatic approach, that I have termed "integrative psychosomatics", at the crossroads of psychoanalysis, medicine, and the neurosciences. Over the years, I returned to Wilhelm Reich's prescient reflections:

> Professor Freud once remarked that the time would come when the organic basis of psycho-analysis would be established ... he postulated a physical element as the nucleus of the neuroses and as the essence of affect ... Naturally we agree with Professor Freud that the interest of science must be decisive on this point, but it is just from this point of view that it appears to us that psycho-analysis cannot be too closely associated with medicine.
>
> One only has to think of the immense field of organic neuroses, hypochondria, neurasthenia, the psychoses ... In our opinion neither science nor the patient would benefit by such a division; there would still be physicians who knew nothing of the soul and psychologists who knew nothing of the body ... The physician would understand the analyst even less than at present, the analyst would again completely forget that the "libido" has a physical (endocrinological) root and a biological function ... That members of the medical profession have shown such an unworthy and unreasoning attitude towards psycho-analysis is not due to the physical preoccupation of their education but is to be attributed to their complexes ... We can condemn the complex-conditioned lack of insight of physicians, but we need not on this account turn our back upon medicine. (Reich, 1927, pp. 253–254)[2]

It has been my resolve and my educational and scientific objective to gain acceptance, despite the considerable resistance in medical circles that continues to this day, for the existence of a psychic apparatus or system (Freud) alongside the various somatic systems—the central nervous system, autonomic nervous system, immune system, and genetic system—I have called this new theoretical approach "the theory of the five systems" or "integrative psychosomatics". I think that psychoanalytic circles are also resistant in their observations of somatic patients because medical and neuroscientific dimensions are not taken into consideration in their clinical case reports, whereas Sigmund Freud, the founder of psychoanalysis, asked himself numerous questions about the relations between the psychic apparatus and the central nervous system that he was seeking to explain.

I asked myself many questions about the very term "psychosomatics", the psyche–soma relations, the approaches developed in psychoanalytically-inspired psychosomatics, and the approaches to psychosomatic medicine developed in the United States and Germany. How could we explain "somatisations"? How could we explain illnesses? How could we explain the role of medicine in connection with psychoanalysis and the role of psychoanalysis in connection with medicine? All of these questions were jostling in my mind, and I spent nearly ten years (from 1993 to 2003) in solitary study of all the key texts of psychoanalysis and psychosomatics, observing patients while exploring their pathologies in medical books and articles to find answers to my questions. My companions on this journey included Sigmund Freud, Pierre Marty, Sándor Ferenczi, Michael Balint, Melanie Klein, André Green, and Winnicott, and I was in a daily dialogue with them all. I sought answers to my questions, and if no answer emerged I looked for a "new way of framing the problem", which led to my psychosomatic meta-model.

In my view, the concept of somatisation poses a problem; it goes back to the translation of psychic disorders into somatic disorders as a development of psychosomatic theory that followed on from Freud's discovery of conversion hysteria; somatising conflicts, mourning, fears, anxiety, and so on.

> Without referring to […] disease, we sometimes somatise, that is we fall more or less seriously physically ill because everything in us is rebelling even without our knowing it, even if we are accepting the ordeal intellectually. (Dolto and Severin, 1982, p. 159)

Somatisation is an "unconscious process that attempts to transfer and transform emotional difficulties into functional somatic problems: headaches, migraines, dysphagia, rheumatism, eczema and so on" (Ancelin-Schützenberger, 1982). This concept of somatisation does not explain illness; it attempts to describe a process using psychoanalytic concepts. As I will show later, Marty's approach to explaining somatisations is principally based on malfunctionings of the mental apparatus and mentalisation in patients; the questions that I will put to Marty now are: how can illness, which is part of medicine, be explained by psychoanalysis? Is there no epistemological limit to your explanations? How can you move from the functioning of the psychic apparatus to physiological and biological disorders? In fact, Marty realised that there were gaps in the psychoanalytic explanations, and he proposed a theoretical model based on vitalism. Drawing on the economic dimension, his model, inspired by evolutionary theory, is an impressive construction of progressive unities that constitute the various psychic organisations of the patients he observed. These increasingly vast unities are reassembled into chains: the central progressive chain of fixations to which correspond major regression, lateral chains, and parallel dynamisms (Marty, 1976, pp. 137–157). This construction does not accord with medical, genetic, and biological research on human development; the biological and neuronal integration processes conform to various programmes in the constitution of progressive chains. This involves structuring the various levels of the living organism, which is the fundamental objective of these programmes that are temporally activated according to sequences that are predefined by the developmental genes. Unlike Freud, Marty did not wonder about psyche–soma relations. I think he realised that his model was provisional, as the following statement shows:

> The concepts of laterality and parallelism are also probably provisional. However, they will only become dispensable when a more appropriate economic conception than our own, perhaps with a broader foundation in a better developed perspective, can explain all the phenomena of human functioning in a way that is ultimately simpler. (Marty, 1976, p. 157)

Vitalist philosophy has now been superseded and cannot serve as a scientific basis for the psychosomatic model that has been developed.

For me, Freud's psychoanalysis is the model of the apparatus for thinking that should be considered in terms of its functioning or hypofunctioning in connection with illness. However, in observing hospital patients, I felt that this first formulation was inadequate, for how can what is happening in a human body—its organs and somatic functioning—be explained using a model of psychic functioning, even if this model refers to the "psychisation" of the body? What happens when the body is very young or not psychised?

In every era, and in fact since Anaxagoras, philosophers, then doctors, and then, from the early twentieth century, psychoanalysts, have pondered at length the relations between mind and body. Throughout the last two and a half millennia, priority has sometimes been given to the mind, to its omnipotence that can cause illnesses, or the body's functioning has been privileged while the mind has been diminished in importance or entirely dismissed as too difficult to determine in quantitative terms: only somatic symptoms (organs and functions) had to be considered for treatment in view of a probable "cure". Today's "evidence-based medicine" completely ignores the existence of a psychic apparatus that is made even more difficult to understand in its functioning by being described in qualitative rather than quantitative terms.

I will now briefly review the scientific advances made by our predecessors.

Historical and clinical outline

At the outset of their investigations, Western psychosomaticians referred to the approach taken by Anaxagoras (500–428 BC) to determine the relations between the psyche (soul) and soma (body); by postulating the two terms of this dichotomy in the human being, Greek thinkers had a profound influence on the development of what Heinroth, an Austrian internist and psychiatrist, termed "psychosomatics" (1815) at the beginning of the nineteenth century.

Through my culture of origin, I have always known that Middle Eastern (Pharaonic Egyptian, Jewish, Arab) and Far Eastern medicine (Chinese, Hindu, Japanese) had taken a unified conception of the human being from earliest antiquity. Studying the works of Hippocrates, who founded the School of Cos, I observed that he understood the human being in its entirety, unlike his colleagues in the School of Cnidos, who emphasised the body's organs and functions, and were the forerunners of the allopathic mechanistic medicine that is familiar to us now. But who still reads Hippocrates, the first of the psychosomaticians? Consequently, from the beginning of the ages, disagreements emerged without actually putting in question the earliest hypotheses—namely, the psyche–soma dichotomy. No Western thinker has cast doubt on this postulate.

How can this enigma of psyche–soma relations be resolved?

Since this distant era, philosophers and doctors have suggested some answers to this philosophical and medical enigma; ever since the Middle Ages and, more recently, Pinel, Broussais, Laennec, and Trousseau, they have all emphasised the role of emotion in somatic disorders. "We all know", wrote Trousseau (1801–1867), "that a slightly strong emotion will suspend the [digestive process] and lead to indigestion; we all know what a fatal impact long-term mental worries have on the digestive system …" (Haynal & Pasini, 1984, p. 15). In his nosography (1798), Pinel (1755–1826) discusses "neuroses of digestion" and "neuroses of circulation". Over the ages, dualistic theories have alternated with monistic theories, supplemented by materialistic theories that regarded the body as the only reality. All of these thinkers certainly felt that there was an enigma to resolve, but they did not yet possess the conceptual tools for analysing the psyche.

Freud laid the scientific foundations that were required for understanding the functioning of the psyche; namely the existence of a mental apparatus (previously the psyche) with connections to the body that remained to be explored. For the first time in two and a half millennia there was finally a model of the psyche's development and functioning: metapsychology. A scientific approach to the problem was possible, but there was still a long way to go; metaphysics was being abandoned and the soul was becoming a psychic apparatus with functioning that formed part of a psychosexual maturation process.

How were the relations between the psychic apparatus and the body to be explained? And illnesses and "somatisation processes"? It was necessary to discover the origin of psychic factors and their role in illnesses. To defend the long-term interests of psychoanalysis, Freud stated in 1923 that he was aware of the existence of psychogenic factors in illnesses, but that he preferred psychoanalysts to limit their field of knowledge to the neuroses. This was a crucial year for the future of psychoanalysis, and Freud's concerns in this period are understandable because, as an institution, psychoanalysis was riven by conflicts—hence his strict emphasis on the neuroses and the training of young psychoanalysts. The recommendation then was to remain within the psychic domain of the neuroses.

The Nazi threat resulted in many doctor-psychoanalysts in Vienna and Berlin emigrating to the United States; this is how Félix Deutsch, with his colleagues such as Franz Alexander (the founder of the Chicago School), Flanders Dunbar, Max Schur, and Thomas Benedek introduced into this country the psychosomatics that went on to flourish. Today, psychosomatic medicine is taught in medical faculties, and American hospitals have departments of psychosomatic medicine.

The psychosomatics movement resumed in Europe after the end of the Second World War with the development of what was known as the Paris School, founded by the doctors Pierre Marty, Michel Fain, Michel de M'Uzan, and Christian David. It is fair to say that since Freud's creation of psychoanalysis, only Pierre Marty, in France, attempted to develop a new model of mental functioning that integrated psychoanalysis into the psychosomatic approach, while the best-known and most famous psychoanalytic authors, Melanie Klein, Anna Freud, Meltzer, Winnicott, Bion, Green, and so on, instead contributed to major developments in contemporary psychoanalytic concepts.

When founding the Chicago School in 1952, Franz Alexander put forward a first explanation of somatisations: for him, there were two types of psychosomatic illness: the expression of blocked aggressive hostile tendencies (e.g., fight or flight) that are not being translated into manifest behaviour, and the expression of inhibited tendencies to dependence and the search for support. Chronic visceral responses lead to disorders of the visceral functions, which enabled Alexander to ascertain seven illnesses that were termed psychosomatic: bronchial asthma, rheumatoid arthritis, ulcerative colitis, essential hypertension, neurodermatitis, thyrotoxicosis (e.g., Graves disease, thyroid hormone imbalances), and gastric and duodenal ulcers; they are also called the "Chicago Seven" in reference to the institute founded by Alexander.

Alexander's approach did not seem to explain all the disorders that were termed psychosomatic because not all somatic disorders in medicine were taken into consideration by this single theory, the so-called specificity theory. Some other theoreticians (Grace & Graham, 1952;

Wolf, 1950) emphasised the importance of life events and their role in illnesses with diverse aetiologies; it was therefore necessary to consider non-specific factors that played a role in maintaining health and the onset of illness. This approach led to a stronger orientation towards developing physiological and psychophysiological approaches. Cannon and Selye demonstrated, in experimental studies, that chronic emotional stimuli—just like toxins or infectious agents—could lead to functional disorders and organic lesions. We are thus confronted with the first biological psychosomatic model that investigates the regulation of the hypothalamic axis, the autonomic nervous system, and the neuroendocrine system. These works are the precursors of American psychosomatic medicine as a medical movement that predominantly considers biological variables, in conjunction with behavioural variables, as well as patients' emotional expression.

However, in this approach, the psychic apparatus is no longer included; the focus is on behaviours and emotions without any reference to mental representations. The psychoanalytic approach of Franz Alexander, of the Hungarian school of psychoanalysis, seems to have disappeared from the contemporary neurophysiological approach, as is confirmed by many North American authors who have been concerned about the disappearance of psychoanalytically-based psychosomatic medicine since 1985.

In fact, American psychoanalysts had put forward a new psychoanalytic approach to psychosomatic illness; Félix Deutsch developed an associative anamnestic method, from which Marty's investigative method was also derived. From the 1940s and 1950s, Margolin (1942), Kubie (Margolin & Kubie, 1944a, 1994b),[3] and Grinker emphasised a psychic regression resulting from ego deficiencies in somatic patients that leads to a "re-somatisation" process involving a temporary disappearance of the psychic apparatus—an idea that is also found in the theory of the French school. This is a process of psychic malfunctioning that facilitates a return of libido into the soma. This concept was developed by Max Schur, Freud's doctor, who treated him until the end of his days. For Schur, under the impact of stress and the reactivation of unconscious conflicts, patients regress in their mode of thinking from secondary processes to primary processes (i.e. symbolism, regressive thought), while the re-somatisation of their responses occurs in parallel. Affects are accompanied by somatic changes, such as oscillations in arterial tension, secretion of gastric juices, and so on; essentially, there is a gradual detachment from psychic life. For

Margolin, the matrix of psychosomatic disorders is established from the earliest months of life. Illness is a regression to a phase of insufficient differentiation between the biological and the psychic. The severe psychosomatic illnesses are situated at the fixation-regression point of the pregenital period, as they are for the French school; this is an "organic" psychosis; psychosomatic patients move between neurosis and psychosis.

Szondi[4] puts forward a profile of the psychosomatic patient: sexual immaturity, pregenitality, persistence of very strong oral and/or anal needs, a highly dependent relationship to the object, failure of the oedipal problematic, and fixation in a binary form of relationship; the patient has rigid mental defences and seems submissive to reality and the social environment (negation and projection are the forms of defence). For Szondi, somatisation is therefore a breakdown of the subject.

Helen Flanders Dunbar (1902–1959), an American, unlike the founding fathers of psychosomatics with their European (primarily Hungarian) origins, became the first president of the North American Society of Psychosomatic Medicine. She suggested composing a specific personality profile with a predisposition towards specific psychosomatic illnesses, such as those associated with road accidents, angina, heart-attacks, and so on, in order to make connections between a psychological profile and a psychosomatic illness.

Thure von Uexküll: the concept of Umwelt

All of the above North American works were written between the 1930s and the 1950s. In continental Europe, the psychosomatic movement developed strongly in Germany and Northern Europe after the end of the Second World War. I should say that my thought has also been influenced by Thure von Uexküll and Ludwig von Bertalanffy. My colleague and friend, Professor Wolfgang Rapp, Emeritus Professor of Psychosomatic Medicine at Heidelberg University, introduced me to the works of Thure von Uexküll (1908–2004) fifteen years ago. Thure von Uexküll was an internist and specialist in psychosomatic medicine, and he created a new way forward by establishing the theoretical foundations of psychosomatic medicine. To do this, he followed the path traced by his famous father, Jakob von Uexküll (1864–1940); this great biologist's main concepts can be found in his book, *Theoretical Biology* (1926), which pursued the scientific objective of reintroducing the autonomous organism as the central subject of the life sciences, thereby making human subjectivity the object of a scientific method. In taking that view, he concurred with the thought of Victor von Weizsäcker, the scion of a family of politicians and theologians who provided a philosophical, anthropological, and clinical basis for psychosomatic medicine. He also maintained a correspondence with Sigmund Freud. Thanks to von Weizsäcker and, after 1945, Victor Frankl, the person and their spirituality regained a central place in patient care, and in the articulation of the second paradigm of medicine put forward by German psychosomaticians. Jakob von Uexküll strongly influenced the development of the biology of organisms and Ludwig von Bertalanffy's systems theory. He studied, in particular, the neurophysiology of the movements of invertebrate animals and used the concept of the "functional cycle" to illustrate behaviour as a regular process, which was a precursor of the cybernetic models that were developed later. He also used semiotics in the biological approach. For him, the capacities and behaviours of animals are founded on signal-based processes; that is to say, the transmission and perception of signals are signifiers of communication and behaviours. As a scientist, Uexküll contributed to the science of development and to epigenetics in biology. He strongly recommended going beyond causality (in the strict sense) in exploring the laws of living matter; in his view, biology had to study organisms not as material objects but as *active subjects*, developing capacities to integrate themselves actively in a complex environment. Consequently, he thought that biology ought to study holistic entities, the objective being to establish a broader perspective than physiology alone, in order to understand the interactive utility of the organism and the world it perceives and inhabits. The organism is therefore an entity that is unified with its surroundings; to describe this entity, Jakob von Uexküll introduced the term *Umwelt* (environment). This is the concept that I have used in my methodological approach, which emphasises the patient's relationship with his family and professional environment, his own "Umwelt".

Thure von Uexküll, Jakob's son, was primarily interested in internal medicine, psychosomatic medicine, philosophy, and semiotics. His work on analysing the fundamental questions of semiotics comprises a study of the interpretation of the "Self"; in this way, he developed a theory of natural semiotic levels, starting from the cell as a "semiotic atom", progressing through all the levels of the living organism to the semantics of human signs, such as language, giving human beings the capacity to represent absent objects and an infinity of possible worlds. His semiotic approach to psychosomatic medicine led him to develop an integrated theory of medicine and subjective anatomy. He criticised medical practice for its "myopic" tendency to concentrate exclusively on the symptomatic aspects of illness, while denying the symbolic importance of each patient's different levels of representation. It is Thure von Uexküll's approach that has inspired me in putting forward the second paradigm of medicine: as he stated, medicine must replace its mechanical model of the body with a model of living systems. Living systems do not react mechanically to "inputs"; they tend to transform the inputs from their environment using their receptors into signals that inform the body's systems of the meaning of the needs that can satisfy them in their environment. These signals make the living systems capable of recognising and assimilating the resources of their environment in order to maintain their autopoiesis as the basis of their health (Uexküll, 1997).

Pierre Marty and the Paris School

In the early 1960s, in France, the Paris School began to develop a new psychosomatic approach that was initiated by Pierre Marty, who sometimes refers in his work to Mustapha Ziwar,[5] an Egyptian member of the Paris Psychoanalytical Society, as a source of inspiration. I think Ziwar's Egyptian origin is important here because it relates back, as I stated above, to a different conception of the human being and his health and illness, and I do not actually know exactly what Mustapha Ziwar's influence on Pierre Marty was.

I think that medical and psychoanalytic contributions of the North American scholars have unquestionably had an influence on the French school's approach. At the beginning of the 1960s, the members of that school developed, in just over twenty years, a major theoretical and clinical corpus that drew mainly on Freud's metapsychological model. However, this was not exclusive, as Marty refers to the vitalist philosophy movement (see above) for his psychosomatic model, hence the title of his book *Les Mouvements Individuels de Vie et de Mort* (The individual movements of life and death), which diverges from the concept of the drives in Freud's metapsychology.

Marty[6] was president of the Paris Psychoanalytical Society during his career; he created a new analytically-based psychosomatic model, one component of which is the metapsychology. All Marty's theoretical contributions are essentially based on the clinical experience that he began to develop in the early 1950s when treating patients who presented with cephalalgias and rachialgias for which it had been impossible to establish any "objective" cause. Marty concisely summarised his findings as *a painful inhibition of thought*. He gradually ascertained that there was a *lack of mental elaboration*. His study of cephalalgic disorders gradually led him to connect these with the cephalo-caudal axis that includes ocular motricity, which seemed to be the site of a regression that was being carried out according to evolutionary theory; this reference to evolutionary theory distanced him from the Freudian approach to the "drive", as I indicated above, the issue being the investigation of the movement that animates psychic life. I will shortly return to this point, which Marty developed substantially in two major works: *Les Mouvements Individuels de Vie et de Mort* and *L'ordre Psychosomatique* (The psychosomatic order). He continued his work with the pioneers of the Paris School from 1957 to 1963, which was completed with the publication of *L'investigation psychosomatique* (The psychosomatic investigation), before pursuing his path by founding the Institute of Psychosomatics (IPSO) with his brother-in-law, Dr Michel Fain, in 1972. For him, this involved an overtly monistic undertaking in comparison with the previous dualism, in reference to the classical dualist psyche–soma approach of Alexander's North American school. Marty's training as a neurosurgeon (he had belonged to a team of neurosurgeons at the end of the Second World War) led him to adopt Hughlings Jackson's theory of "disinvolution", according to which the neural functions that develop last are the first to be destroyed. It is likely that this neurological theory influenced the concept of *progressive disorganisation* and that his emphasis on *evolutionary principles* led to his construction of the architecture of the living organism, which he conceived as a hierarchical system of increasingly integrated functional organisations. To supply these functional unities, he referred to a unique, *vital* energy that powered the life drives, privileging unconscious economic processes and thus leading psychosomatics into problematics that no longer belonged to the classical neurotic model developed by psychoanalysis. In this respect, he departed from the concepts of the libido, drives, and narcissism without actually removing them from the observation of patients. Unlike Alexander, he therefore does not resort to an understanding of somatic symptoms based on psychic conflicts; for him, as for Freud, it is the excessive sensory and motor excitation that leads to the mental regulation processes being overwhelmed in a way that ultimately breaks down the psychosomatic homeostasis.

According to Marty, mystery surrounds the life drives and the death drives because nothing is known about the origin and their state; death is parallel to life, and "the death drives generally contribute more to the individual structural formation than to the individual's deep disorganisation" (Marty, 1976, p. 125). To explain this point, he puts forward the hypothesis of fixation-regression points established by the life drives during phylogenesis and ontogenesis. When a trauma prevents the achievement of the most evolved functional organisation, it gives way to disorganisations by the death drives. In this respect, Marty's vision is very different from the approach to the death drive developed by Freud; this is a major advance on the dualistic theory of the drives. It is now easier to understand the architectural construction of Marty's model that draws on a progredient and hierarchised integration of somatic functions that gradually converge in the context of a central fasciculus towards the most highly-developed point (i.e. the mentally-developed point). This developmental point makes reference to the oedipal mental organisation. It is not a matter of intellectual functioning as in Jackson's model; *any psychic malfunctioning can lead to a somatic disorder.*

As Catherine Parat stated: "… unlike the development that started from the beginning of life, the disorganisation of thought in its abundance could, in a regredient movement, gradually attack the somatopsychic organisation to the point of death if adequately constituted levels of fixation did not stop the counter-progressive movement" (1994, p. 25).

Marty's emphasis on the confirmed insufficiency of mental functioning led him to develop some new nosographic concepts: operative thinking, essential depression, and progressive disorganisation. The concept of operative thinking, which was developed with Michel de M'Uzan makes reference to a conscious thinking

> … unconnected with any discernible (representative) fantasy movements … Operative thinking does not use neurotic or psychotic mental mechanisms … This thought, however, by attaching itself to things rather than abstract concepts, products of the imagination or symbolic expressions, suggests that the connection with

> words is precarious and thus suggests a process of cathexis at the archaic level. (1976, p. 125)

Marty then introduced the concept of "operative life" that replaced the concept of operative thinking to "take better account of the reduction in thought with regard to the importance of behaviours" (1976, pp. 133–134).

At this point, I must draw attention to the simultaneity of psychosomatic discoveries on both sides of the Atlantic; in Boston, Professor Sifnéos and Dr Némiah (1970) put forward the concept of alexithymia to define the same clinical data. Alexithymia and operative thinking are identical concepts: alexithymia emphasises more specifically the patient's lack of words to describe what he is feeling—with alexithymia, we are dealing with observations of patients expressing their emotions.

To clarify his thinking on psychic dysfunction, Marty refers back to the concept of the preconscious from Freud's first topography. He considers the preconscious to be "the turntable of the psychosomatic economy", and closely examines the density and abundance of mental representations and the fluidity of the preconscious in order to evaluate the mental capacities of patients with regard to the illness, therefore determining points of vulnerability–defence. This approach has made it possible to reconsider highly intellectual patients so that the psychotherapist does not hastily present a psychoanalytic indication that might be detrimental to them—not confusing high intellectual level with "mentalisation", which is weakness and impoverishment of the mental associative capacities.

I will return throughout this book to Marty's many clinical concepts, which I still use when investigating somatic patients. The study of operative life led him to put forward hypotheses concerning the earliest stages of the individual unconscious; in the unconscious conceived as a "first mosaic" there are two functional principles:

> … on the one hand, a principle of automation and iteration, principle of repetition (of a state) that maintains, in a relatively stagnant way, all forms of psychosomatic functioning; on the other hand, a principle of programming (introduction to the programme and its instigation), which would especially open the progressive path to the various functional connections and associations,

to hierarchical systems … to development, that is to the programme of organisations and reorganisations. (1990, pp. 35–36)

This particular form of Marty's thought led him to devise a method of "psychosomatic classification" for forming a diagnosis according to a new nosography, to be used in our dealings with the social security authorities for communicating to them the data from our work in hospital; this methodological tool was also used in training future psychosomaticians. From 1986, I began to work with him on epidemiological research, using the psychosomatic classification. This method makes it possible to collect data for each patient concerning his psychic functioning (structure) and major habitual features, bringing together symptomatic data, usual lifestyle, former anamnestic data, and major current characteristics (immediate symptomatic data and recent anamnestic data). Marty attached great importance to research that would help to advance the psychoanalytically-based psychosomatic discipline that he had developed. I should mention that I published two pieces of research with him (Marty et al., 1987; Marty & Stora, 1988, 1989; Stora et al., 1989),[7] along with two others that, sadly, could not be attributed to him as they were published posthumously. I have always thought that it was necessary in a discipline such as psychosomatics to have a method allowing epidemiological studies to be developed, which is contrary to psychoanalytic practices as they have developed in the psychoanalytic institutes of the International Psychoanalytical Association. It should never be forgotten that Freud himself used statistical studies concerning his patients in his early works.

Since the death of my teacher and friend, I have therefore continued to develop this method that has since become a new method because I do not know how it would have validated the work that I have been carrying out since the end of 1993 at La Pitié-Salpêtrière. This new method (cf. Appendix) returns to the metapsychological model (object relationship, narcissism etc.), incorporating all of the most important contributions of psychoanalysts since Freud, as well as a medical nosography (making reference to the International Classification of Diseases) and the neurosciences. I have called it the "Method of assessing psychosomatic risk", and employ it for the purpose of individual diagnosis, but also for epidemiological studies that integrate qualitative (psychic) variables and quantitative, biological variables into a general model.

This method provides a scientific basis for research in integrative psychosomatics.

Why integrative psychosomatics?

For a long time, I pushed aside some questions that I was asking myself about Marty's explanation of the somatisation process. As I stated above, there was a theoretical and clinical gap: for Marty, we deal with a high quantum of excitations on a daily basis. There are three available outlets for discharging these excitations:

1. the path of mental elaboration by the psychic apparatus
2. the path of behaviours (discharge in behaviours)
3. the path of "somatisations"; the mental apparatus is overwhelmed following traumas and excitations flow into the somatic apparatuses.

How this happens is never elaborated; it might be inferred that these excitations are transmitted in some way to the soma.

It was therefore in wondering about the destiny of these excitations that I turned to the neurosciences and medicine to answer this question. My first realisation was that it was necessary to cross the epistemological boundary of psychoanalysis, as only other sciences could enable me to resolve such a problem. The model that I developed presents an answer to the following question: when, owing to a constitutional deficiency or a dysfunction, the psychic apparatus cannot elaborate the quantum of excitations, what happens to them? The transmission of mental excitations to the central nervous system and the imbalance in the homeostasis of the other biological systems enables us to perceive every dimension of the problem. I think that concentrating on the interrelations between the psychic and biological processes is the most pertinent approach for understanding patients and explaining illnesses. I should point out that integrative psychosomatics is situated at the crossroads of psychoanalysis, medicine, and the neurosciences (Stora, 2010a).

In what follows, I will be presenting some observations from clinical cases of patients I have treated over the last fifteen years, as well as some sequences from psychosomatic psychotherapies. I am deeply grateful to my patients, because they have helped me to understand their relations to their illnesses, facilitating the therapeutic relationship so that they can be treated more effectively.

This book aims to illustrate this new approach to patients and illnesses, which in a sense is an implementation of the second paradigm of medicine, and of what in my book on neuropsychoanalysis (2011) I termed *neuropsychosomatics*.

INTRODUCTION

"I call heaven and earth to record this day against you, that I have set before you life and death, blessing and cursing: therefore choose life, that both thou and thy seed may live." (Deuteronomy, Chapter Thirty, verse 19)

"The psychosomatician is always on the side of life"

When I arrived at La Pitié-Salpêtrière one Monday morning, I stopped as usual at the entrance barrier; the duty guard was a young North African man from my native town of Constantine. We smiled and greeted each other in Arabic before he raised the barrier. When there are no cars waiting, we often talk and exchange memories. On this occasion, he asked me a favour: no ambulance was available and a young pregnant woman who had come by metro urgently needed to be taken to the maternity ward. This building is right next to mine (the Husson-Mourier building), and I drove her there while wondering about many things that I did not dare ask her. Why had no one come with her? Why had she come by metro instead of by taxi? I let her out quickly at the end of the Avenue de la Nouvelle Pitié, wished her all the best, and went on to my wing: the endocrinology department.

Sometimes we do not receive any answer to our questions.

I am a hospital psychosomatician, and for nearly nineteen years now I have had a practice at La Pitié-Salpêtrière, based in the endocrinology department and attached to the psychiatry department. I often think laughingly about Sigmund Freud's fears that psychoanalysis might be replaced by endocrinology, and I dismiss this fear of the founder of psychoanalysis because it is not justified; how could psychoanalysis ever be replaced by a medical discipline? Nevertheless, some American colleagues who have developed psychosomatic medicine, based on Dr Franz Alexander's work in their country, have moved away from the psychoanalytic approach and gradually replaced it since the 1980s with psycho-neuro-endocrinology, which is supplemented by observation of patients' behaviours. Does this, however, confirm Freud's fears? Analytically-based psychosomatic medicine has been reduced to the practice of a behavioural medicine, but psychoanalysis has not disappeared. Is it possible to develop a new psychosomatic approach in the twenty-first century while preserving the psychoanalytic dimension? This is my exact purpose in this book.

Since my earliest childhood I have been attracted by the mystery of illnesses. When I was ten years old, my paternal grandfather, a true Mediterranean patriarchal family head, developed cancer. This was right in the middle of the Second World War, and there were many reasons to be anxious on a daily basis. This strange illness that frightened all the family members both worried and fascinated me; adults paid little attention to children then, and I had a great deal of time to observe. This gift for observation is very useful for me today when I am talking with patients.

I often looked at my beloved grandfather and experienced at second hand, the progress of the treatments and the development of his illness. He seemed to cope courageously, and I never saw him express any kind of suffering, and yet I could sense it. He spent his days in one room of the house reading, according to tradition, the psalms of David to help him through this period of his life. I never spoke to him, and he never uttered a word to me either; we just looked at each other. When I am with my patients today, I think I still have this look.

The limits of allopathic medicine had been reached, and the family members seemed to be in a panic but I did not understand the underlying reasons for this; in fact, I sensed the fear of death, but in Mediterranean civilisation, this is a word that is not uttered from fear of it occurring in consequence. A great deal of anxiety was being communicated to me, and death was deeply present there; in the last resort, recourse was made to "witchcraft" practices that were familiar to me because I feared their associated mysteries, especially the rituals.

How could a family, perfectly assimilated into French culture, turn to what Tobie Nathan calls the "invisible beings"—the spirits that threaten and help human beings? It was much later in my studies of ethnopsychoanalysis, with my friend and colleague Tobie Nathan, that I developed my knowledge of the traditional therapies of the world's peoples. During my childhood, I was immersed in what in the West is called magical thinking, which was condemned by the religion of Moses, and severely criticised by rationalist thinking. "The witches" came one day with their drums to drive away the spirits imprisoned in my grandfather's body, but their actions failed; my grandfather died of his cancer. Confronted with death for the first time, I coped by turning to God and religion, with its rituals that allow the acceptance of death, whereas later in my clinical experience I very often became aware of my patients' denial of mourning and its traumatic effects on their health.

I wanted to fulfil my obligations towards my grandfather, so, with members of my family, I carried him to his tomb at the cemetery, which I remember was situated in the highest part of the town, across the suspension bridge that spanned the terrifying, dizzying precipice of the Rummel's gorges. The tradition then was for men to bear the coffin of the deceased on their shoulders. I was sadly following the procession when I noticed the fatigue of those who were carrying my grandfather's coffin, so I went up to take the place of a man who was tired. I was only a twelve-year-old child, and the coffin was sinking painfully into my shoulder, but I clung on to pay tribute to a man who was the head of my family, who often frightened me when exercising his authority, but whom I have since come to regard benevolently and affectionately.

These two events—the visit from the "witch doctors" and my grandfather's death—deeply influenced my desire to care for my fellow human beings. I was already asking myself many questions about medical practices and their efficacy, as well as about the strangeness of what are now called traditional therapies. Like doctors, the psychoanalyst psychosomatician encounters death in his daily practice, which is rarely the case for a psychoanalyst.

The construction of a new psychosomatic approach owes a great deal to my teachers at the Aumale lycée in Constantine, such as the philosophy teacher who strongly encouraged us to read and re-read Sigmund Freud's *Introductory Lectures on Psychoanalysis*, a book that I still have in my library today, which led me to undertake training in psychoanalysis;[1] or the physics and chemistry teacher, who guided my reading towards Albert Einstein and the theory of relativity. I applied myself very assiduously to reading this work that I found hard to understand, but which strongly developed my curiosity about the theories in physics concerning the constitution of the universe. This scientific dimension has been present throughout my studies and continues to this day. Although I did not then have the mathematical knowledge to understand such complex theory, I turned to instead to Einstein's philosophical writings; these have guided me throughout my career, and I have always enjoyed exploring the mystery of existence:

> The most beautiful experience we can have is the mysterious. It is the fundamental emotion that stands at the cradle of true art and true science. Whoever does not know it and can no longer wonder, no longer marvel, is as good as dead, and his eyes are dimmed. It was the experience of mystery—even if mixed with fear—that engendered religion. A knowledge of the existence of something we cannot penetrate, our perceptions of the profoundest reason and the most radiant beauty, which only in their most primitive forms are accessible to our minds: it is this knowledge and this emotion that constitute true religiosity. In this sense, and only this sense, I am a deeply religious man … I am satisfied with the mystery of life's eternity and with a knowledge, a sense, of the marvelous structure of existence—as well as the humble attempt to understand even a tiny portion of the Reason that manifests itself in nature. (Albert Einstein, quoted in Jammer, 2011, pp. 73–74)

The exploration of the mystery of the human being has been the guiding theme of my scientific career, and something that I have developed through my training as a psychoanalyst and a psychosomatician. The scientific and spiritual dimensions have always been deeply interrelated in all my investigations.

The constitutive elements of an identity and the personality are fundamental to explaining our being in the world (the self); throughout my life, I have tried to bring together and unify these parts of myself. The French culture I learnt at school and university constitutes the intellectual component of my personality, to which I must add the

Judaeo–Arab and Judaeo–Berber cultures that are its foundations. The latter two have determined my value system, emotions, and behaviour; during my law studies, I supplemented my knowledge of Islam by specialising in Islamic law. At the time, I was one of only five students taking the classes, given by a famous law professor from Algiers. My family lived in the Berber and Arab-Muslim worlds for centuries, and I have never abandoned these values that were transmitted to me, which, along with French culture, have deeply influenced my world view. The problem has been accepting them at the deepest level of myself in order to gain acceptance for them in my intellectual environment.

When I was beginning to learn about psychoanalytic psychosomatics with Pierre Marty, the founder of the Paris School, I adopted his approach to the problems without ever questioning his teaching, in accordance with the ideal of identification and obedience to teachers in my world of origin. Nevertheless, I asked myself many questions after I had studied the theoretical approaches of psychosomaticians in past centuries and up to the twentieth century. It is difficult to criticise one's teachers without ever putting them totally in question, while pursuing the objective of advancing knowledge and skill by attempting to follow the path that they have taken. That is, nevertheless, how I proceeded.

Before I go on to detail the clinical cases drawn from my psychosomatic practice, I will return to describing my hospital day, because I have to attend to patients in my department.

Several years ago, following a restructuring of the department, I was assigned to the metabolic syndrome unit, which is run by a young clinical director who is very open to psychosomatics. I begin my day by greeting the secretary of our unit, then I walk past the nurses' room, where they are preparing the material for the day, and they wave at me from a distance. Finally, on my left, I pass the room used by the interns and external doctors who, also, are busy reading the files of the patients we are shortly going to receive. The consultation no longer takes place in the main building where I have my office, so I go to the nurses' room, where they kindly greet me with my two trainee students. There is not enough space yet for the psychosomatician; does this reflect the difficulty of recognising this approach?

Whereas the young interns and external doctors ask me few questions after my clinical interviews, the nurses want to know about the outcome of my conversations; they often compare my conclusions with their own observations in order to amplify them. They have intuitively incorporated the patient's *subjective dimension*: they treat patients rather than illnesses. Because of their training, the young doctors concentrate on the biological factors that are printed on endless pages. They pursue precise treatment objectives and, as they cannot devote much time to listening to patients, they concentrate on the symptoms and measurement of the biological factors. The account of the patient's life events is our only common reference point, but not always. They do not wonder about the patient's relationship with his illness, that is to say his mental representation of the illness; similarly, they do not wonder about his capacity for therapeutic observance or his quality of life. I think that the emphasis on the technical factors, albeit necessary, diverts them from a deep relationship with the patient, with the patient as a subject, as if our medicine no longer knew how to investigate patients. In this sense, they are still applying what I call the "first paradigm of medicine".

My colleagues have made considerable efforts to accept a psychosomatic practice that they allow to supplement the medical consultation, with my name appearing on the board so that, just like the doctors, I can meet all the patients who have come to consult us. This is the only department of La Pitié-Salpêtrière, to my knowledge, in which psychosomatician and doctors work side by side. Strangely, patients never raise any problem about receiving me; they do not equate psychosomatics with mental illness. They intuitively suppose that it concerns relations between mind and body—above all, they want to talk, which I observe at every meeting, to someone who listens to and tries to understand them without judging.

In contrast to Pierre Marty's practice, I allow only one student at my side in my consultation. In the 1960s, eight to ten psychosomatics students attended his consultations; this teaching system, a legacy of Charcot's tradition, always made me uneasy throughout my psychoanalytic and psychosomatic training. How is it possible to converse with a patient when there are so many people present? What is the influence of such an arrangement on the patient's psychic functioning?

I have since abandoned this cumbersome arrangement, with its unpredictable effect on the patient's mental functioning; moreover, no hospital room in our department can accommodate so many people, although, at the medical level, the "grand visit" (professor with students) continues its course.

In my current practice, I only see the patient once, and this single investigation must allow the patient's psychosomatic functioning (for risk associated with insufficiency of mental functioning), and his capacity to follow medical recommendations, such as medication, diet, physical activity etc., to be assessed. This is a difficult task; how can enough information be obtained in so little time to help the patient in the treatment of his illness? To complete our observation, we can see the patient again in three months when he returns for a further check-up, which gives some reassurance.

In my clinical classes and consultations, I often recommend using the following guidelines, which were developed, with some variations, by the first great "psychosomatics" teacher,[2] Dr Sándor Ferenczi:

- adopt an empathic and warm attitude
- engage in a dialogue
- do not leave the patient in silence
- answer his questions.

In therapy and psychosomatic practice, the psychosomatician adopts a maternal attitude, so as to approach the patient closely in order to understand him better.

I often tell my students that, with a somatic patient, we must create in ourselves *an empathically welcoming mental space* that facilitates access to unconscious expressions; we must capture the smallest details of behaviour and emotional manifestations and interpret them for ourselves. It is important to give ourselves a long time to reflect—using mental elaboration—before forming any psychosomatic hypotheses. It goes without saying that, with clinical experience, this period of reflection can be shortened. We must quickly gain access to our own associations of ideas in order to lend the patient "our apparatus for dealing with thoughts" (Bion, 1962) if his own is presently inadequate. We have to be available and free, as far as possible, of personal problems that can divert us from listening to the patient.

I join my two students, who are trainees on the university diploma in psychosomatics, in the nurses' room, where they are beginning to post up the consultation forms; the patients' names, times at which we will be arriving, and so on. I put on my white coat, as I was strongly recommended to do long ago now by my colleagues—they have added a red badge (the doctors' badge) with my name and specialism: psychosomatics. All of this is symbolic, but I know that this appearance identifies me as part of the medical community and can, at the same time, unsettle patients; what do they perceive when I enter their room? How is a relationship of trust to be established in the minimum of time? Is the patient going to say nothing, give minimal information, or talk to us at length about all the treatments received over the last twenty years, in order to adopt a defensive position by talking about his problems rather than himself?

Each person is unique, and with every new patient I have to undertake a new therapeutic "adventure". My thoughts on this are well expressed by Albert Einstein:

> The whole of science is nothing more than a refinement of every day thinking. It is for this reason that the critical thinking of the physicist cannot possibly be restricted to the examination of the concepts of his own specific field. He cannot proceed without considering critically a much more difficult problem, the problem of analyzing the nature of everyday thinking. (1936, p. 59)

Before introducing to you my first patient, Marie-Laure, I will provide you with some reflections on doctor–patient relations, in order to give you a better understanding of current practices, both in hospitals and private practice. I am going to take more inspiration from the example of American working practices that, in some respects, are very different from our own, and in others very similar. The objective here is to improve our medical and therapeutic practices.

Have we lost sight of the patient as a person?

Concerning barriers between doctors and patients, Dr Pauline W. Chen tells us about her hospital experience:

> Several years ago I helped care for a man who had been hospitalised with a severe infection of the abdominal wall. When his primary doctors discovered that the bacteria responsible was resistant to most antibiotics, they quickly isolated him, moving him into a single room with a sign on the door proclaiming "Contact Precautions" and directing visitors to put on gloves, mask and gown before entering. But garbing up in all those items was not a straightforward exercise. The gowns, vast swaths of baby-yellow polyester, added an insulating and sweat-inducing layer. The masks were either so flimsy they fell off easily or so unyielding they muffled voices and steamed up eyeglasses. (2010, p. 1)

It was the same with the gloves, which were intolerable to wear. I myself put on these protective clothes for several years when I was in contact with my patients who had had heart, kidney, or pancreas transplants. I would put on this blue garment that the nurses laughingly called the "Smurfs' outfit".

It is obvious that all these precautions made visits to Dr Chen's patient difficult. Most of the doctors and nursing staff, and even his wife, ended up complaining about having to put on this protective clothing every day. As the weeks passed, the clinicians gradually reduced their interaction with the patient; they ended up instructing one of their junior staff to treat him and take care of sterilising the bedroom. The increasing isolation of the patient led him to withdraw psychologically into himself, from everyone but his spouse. His daily statements about "fighting this illness" became increasingly inaudible, his voice ceased to be anything but a murmur, and finally it disappeared. The patient stopped turning his face towards the doctors every time they called him—he preferred to look and stare at the ceiling. In a sense, I would say that as "the blank in thought" appeared increasingly, the patient regressed and became disorganised.

When his lungs, heart, and finally his kidneys began to malfunction, the patient's room became increasingly full of technical equipment to help him to carry on his life. The small room in which he was confined was transformed into a futuristic space full of machines and plastic tubes; a very noisy and anonymous space, in which only the doctors' faces, covered in yellow masks, appeared. When the patient died of a heart attack two months later, it was difficult to forget the weeks that led up to his death, and it was possible to think only of one thing: by fighting so efficiently against the infection, had we not lost sight of the person?

For nearly half a century, experts in infectious diseases and hospital epidemiologists have been using various precautionary methods for fighting multi-resistant bacteria. These methods—hand-washing, isolation by coats, gloves, masks, and visual protective gear—belong to the routine of hospital life throughout the country; nearly one-quarter of patients in hospital, at one time or another, are the object of protective measures such as those described above. But whereas doctors and patients expect these precautions, the consequences of such measures on the patient's health have never been assessed. Some doctors, from fear of contagion, end up adopting phobic behaviours that are uncontrollable. The fear of contagion overtakes them and they end up wearing gloves and other protective clothes all day. It is obvious that the fear of contagion can severely compromise the quality of care, as studies have demonstrated. Some recent studies have also shown that the patients isolated in this way were suffering from depression and anxiety. Some epidemiological research also points to the negative consequences of such excessive precautions on patients' general health. Doctors wonder how to tell if there will be increasingly more "contact barriers" between them and their patients in the future. Dr Leif Hass, from the Alta Bates Summit medical centre (Oakland), states: "We just have to make sure that in the age of technology and rapid reforms, some of our best tools for healing—simple things like touching people and telling them you care and making them feel you are there for them—don't get lost";[3] this is also the question that I am constantly asking.

Such enquiries into the doctor–patient relationship are frequent, but not sufficiently well-known, and unfortunately they are not taught in our medical faculties. At a conference[4] in 2011 held at La Pitié-Salpêtrière, entitled "Cardiology and Integrative Psychosomatics", Prof Daniel Thomas presented a paper: "Cardiology: when technology dominates the care relationship". In his conclusion, he emphasised the essential dialogue between doctor and patient: "Respecting the patient's autonomy and freedom; allowing the patient to express his priorities, his preferences, and his refusal. It is not possible to "prescribe a form of behaviour"; only a free and motivated personal decision, taken following a positive exchange, has any chance of producing lasting effects". It is desirable that such recommendations of medical practice should be known and widely circulated.

Reviving a dying art: the medical examination

Integrative psychosomatics is, first of all, the art of conducting a clinical examination that will supplement the medical examination itself. This involves a psychoanalytic anamnesis that takes into consideration the dimensions of the patient's psychic functioning, his behavioural manifestations, all the affective expression (emotions and feelings), and, finally the family, professional, and socio-economic environment.[5] Every time I meet a patient and introduce myself, I explain to them that a psychosomatician connects events from their current and past life with the somatic problems from which he is suffering, and that during our conversation, we will also review the somatic problems from which he has suffered throughout his life. I then complete a detailed form to give to the clinicians to enable them to understand better the psychic dimensions that invariably go unnoticed, as understanding this does not form part of their medical training. It is extremely surprising to note that, with every patient, our young doctors are absolutely unprepared for the conversations they will have to conduct; they keep to strictly biological and medical observations as a result of their university education.

I would like to turn once again to the United States, and refer to Dr Abraham Verghese, senior associate chairman at Stanford University. His mission is to revive what is nowadays considered a vanished art—the physical examination of the patient. Art and medicine seem to belong to two separate worlds, states Dr Verghese, but to him they are one and the same. He has "an endless curiosity about people", and asks himself many questions about his patients' lives when they leave the hospital. "People are infinite mysteries"; it seems that the physical examination has totally disappeared because we are living in an age in which doctors use advanced technological equipment and laboratory tests—under great time pressure, they no longer have any time for their patients. Some doctors are very pleased about the disappearance of this type of examination that has been superseded by technology, and think there are more effective ways of spending time with patients. Others admit that they conduct this type of examination only because the patients expect to be examined in that way; "a sort of remnant of a bygone age". Medical faculties in the United States have allowed this type of examination to disappear, and Dr Verghese observes that he has encountered an increasing number of interns who no longer know how to test or feel a patient's reflexes. One of his favourite jokes to tell is that if a patient arrives at hospital with one less finger, the young doctors will insist on doing an in-depth orthopaedic examination and an MRI scan, only to confirm that he really has one less finger. Dr Verghese, who grew up in India and has practised medicine there, knows very well that when sophisticated equipment is scarce or absent, sound professional skills are needed to conduct an in-depth examination that will provide vital information, help decide which type of test to request, and, above all, which type of test not to request—a major consideration in the United States, where healthcare costs dominate medical decisions. "A physical examination therefore fulfils an important ritual function by which two strangers are transformed into doctor and patient." Over the years since he was appointed in 2007, he has developed what is known as "the Stanford 25", which is a list of techniques that every doctor ought to know, such as listening to the heartbeat and so on; for him, this is in fact only the beginning. Dr Verghese seems perplexed by the interest being shown in his work, because the examination techniques that he is suggesting are nothing other than the techniques that he has been using and learning for decades in India.

In his philosophy of approach to the patient, I notice some of Dr Verghese's qualities in his teaching. Surrounded by his third-year medical students, he is followed on the grand visit to the patient in his department, and what is remarkable is the questions he asks himself and puts to his students: "What did you notice on the patient's bedside table? A tray? A book? Any clues that can tell us whether the patient can eat or not, if the patient is active and alert or not? Does the patient seem comfortable? Or does he seem to be suffering?" In addition to the usual medical questions that every professor puts to his students in such visits, this eminent practitioner seeks to develop the medical students' observational skills, as we do in our psychosomatic and psychoanalytic practices. He tells them: "We're going to walk along this corridor where our patients' rooms are and I'm going to ask you if you've noticed anything unusual. I'll ask you some questions about someone I've seen while walking down this corridor. Look carefully at the patients when you walk past their room." He stops to examine the next patient and he points out to the students his signs of facial weakness—an inability to raise his eyebrows, and an eyelid that is slightly higher on one side than the other when he asks the patient if he can examine his teeth. He then puts this question to his students: "When we walked along the corridor, what did you notice about the patient in the next room?" This patient had watched them walking past in the corridor and the professor had noticed that only one of her eyes had moved. Only two or three students had noticed this symptom.

I will not go into further detail about Dr Verghese's practice, and I will emphasise the qualities that are necessary for observing our patients: when I enter a patient's room, I take some time to observe the patient's physical appearance, how he walks, sits down, the objects on the bedside table, the books or newspapers that are being read, the television programme (if the television is on)—all the details that allow me to begin to compile internally a first image of our meeting. In introducing the first patient, I am now going to develop in more detail the specific observations of the clinical examination in integrative psychosomatics.

CHAPTER ONE

Marie-Laure and metabolic syndrome: relations between the psychic apparatus and the hypothalamic axis

Marie-Laure is in a room on my left, halfway along the corridor; when I knock on the door, she greets my student and me with a smile. She is of average height, and wears a loose-fitting jumper. We are, of course, in the metabolic syndrome unit, and most of our patients are here for problems relating to excess weight or obesity, and, therefore, cardiovascular risk. They spend three days in a day hospital to have tests performed and to be given recommendations for treatment, medicine, diet, and physical activity. This is a patient with a pleasant manner who reveals that she takes care of herself. This dimension that we term "narcissistic" in psychoanalysis is often to be considered favourably, with its many meanings: she takes care of herself and does this for herself, or she takes care of herself, and does this for others, or she takes care of herself and does this both for herself and others. In any case, narcissism is a vital current of neonatal origin (Grunberger) that supports the life drives (Marty). The presence of narcissism is a factor in a positive prognosis, but there are some exceptions that will be seen later (death narcissism, Green).

Marie-Laure sits down on the edge of the bed, and immediately begins to talk about her stressful life as a train driver; she talks about her work-related stress, and I imagine her often being overwhelmed by the problems of her exhausting work. She tells me that three months ago she began therapy with a psychiatrist—she sometimes has anxiety attacks. She has been taking Prozac twice daily for several years, and she is finding it extremely difficult to reduce this dose.

I wonder to myself what she wants to say to me, and whether she is she addressing me as a doctor or as a psychosomatician; does she want to establish a relationship of trust by communicating her worries to me? Does she want to stop taking Prozac, and want me to advise her on an appropriate withdrawal procedure, or is she looking in a "transferential" way for approval for some new autonomous behaviour? Obviously, I first ask myself a basic question that is to return with each of the clinical observations: what is the patient's object relationship?[1] What is she repeating with me from this primary relationship? The "object" is—in psychoanalytic theory and practice—the Mother of the earliest period of life, and we all unwittingly repeat this archaic relational behaviour in relationships with others. When the patient looks at me, whom does she see? I am thinking, of course, about the early looks exchanged between mother and child. In her expression, I try to perceive the first look—the maternal reflection, the mirror.

We are gradually going to explore every aspect of her life in order to understand her better.

Marie-Laure has already been to our department last year, and she has managed to lose a small amount of weight; she weighs 88kg and is 1.60m tall, which represents an excess weight that can be reduced by following a diet, or even a change of eating behaviour, and I advise her to speak with our dietician.

I notice once again here that she is seeking my approval in a parental way—she is making some progress and I must encourage her, which I immediately do. She is seeking *approval* for her behaviour in my gaze, which may suggest a relationship to an "ego ideal" to be satisfied; again, I wonder about the nature of her relationship with her mother.

Is the object present in her psyche? I am referring here to Klein's theory concerning the introjection of the maternal object during the first nine months of life.

There seem to be few satisfactions in Marie-Laure's life; this is a fundamental consideration for her long-term equilibrium, and I continue to wonder silently about her capacity to cathect relationships.

I therefore continue asking about her familial, professional, and social relationships in general.

Could Marie-Laure be isolated, in family and social terms? Does she have some friends?

This *economic* dimension is crucial in psychosomatics because it is important to know how a person cathects this *libidinal* energy in his relations and activities, thereby revealing good psychosomatic functioning.

In reply, Marie-Laure talks to me about her two daughters, one of whom is twenty-six-years-old and has already left home; the other is twenty and still lives with her, but is now leading her own life. She tells me that she is anxious about the time when her second daughter will leave her.

What is her second daughter's role? Does her second daughter fulfil the role of a person who helps her to reduce excitations (the role of a maternal protective shield)—that is, a maternal external object? My patient's worry about her daughter's departure raises a question about her capacity to separate from someone she loves and to continue her life by re-cathecting her energy in relationships and activities; she seems helpless.

I begin to construct silently the hypothesis of a psychic fragility in the early period of Marie-Laure's life, but I do not have enough elements yet.

In introducing my psychosomatician's role, I had indicated to Marie-Laure that my work involves establishing the connections between current and past life events and the problems from which she is suffering; this statement enables me to address every aspect of life, with the patient's consent.

The associative thread of the discourse about the family continues. We speak about her husband, whom she tells me she divorced from twenty-one years ago (when she was thirty-three years old), but that he still sees their children. The tone of her voice (i.e., the appearance of an emotion) prompts me to ask her if she believes that she has recovered from her divorce; she confirms to me that she feels she has not yet moved beyond it, which relates back to my above hypotheses about her difficulties in separating from, and "mourning" for, others.

I assess the possible "drive de-fusion" here (life drive/death drive), following the divorce experienced as an abandonment; I think this involves a narcissistic injury, accompanied by a fear of losing the object's love, which is considered by Freud to be a trauma.

After her divorce, she met a man with whom she then lived after her marriage, but, again, life is often cruel; her partner committed suicide seven years ago and she has not yet mourned this.

We can note the quest for an external object to maintain her psychic equilibrium following her divorce; at her partner's death (trauma), Marie-Laure was confronted with mourning the loss of her new object, who died in dramatic circumstances. Her partner had supported her for nearly fourteen years.

It now becomes easier to understand how this empathetic relationship was established from the beginning of the consultation. I, too, am playing the role of a benevolent and reassuring external object, just like the doctors and nurses; I do not have any prerogative in that respect. Marie-Laure needs the other to lead her life.

However, if the object has not been internalised, what is the nature of her relations with the other? Is it a transference relationship that relates back to an oedipal, genital problematic (consequently, the object exists inside the psyche), or is it an attachment relationship of the kind formed in the early stages of life, before the object is internalised in the psyche? I am referring here to the psychoanalytic works of the last twenty years on the object relationship, the clinical treatment of emptiness (Green), deficiencies in mothering in the early stages of life and, above all, infantile neurosis as elaborated by Freud. As Freud taught us, the presence of an infantile neurosis presupposes the oedipal problematic; if we do not establish this presence or if it is hardly there in outline, we are dealing with pregenital problematics, and the attachment relationship (Bowlby, Winnicott) predominates, instead of a transference relationship that has consequently not come about.

Marie-Laure explains to me that her partner was an alcoholic and that he never wanted to seek help for his dependency. I explore my patient's relationships with her parents; she tells me that she does not know the date on which her father died, as if that belonged to a distant past. I continue to wonder silently about her relationship with her father and, as Marie-Laure herself also remains silent, about what Pierre Marty often called "abnormalities of mental functioning"; with a sort of blank in the discourse, I find myself at a crossroads. This is a very important technical problem in psychosomatics and psychoanalysis: what path to follow when the patient's flow of speech stops? Is this attributable to repression, or is it a momentary arrest of thought?

Marie-Laure's silence concealed some thoughts about her relationship with her mother, who was a great and militant feminist with a very turbulent past, having had three children by three different fathers. The object thus comes into view—did Marie-Laure's mother have time to take care of her newborn children?

Marie-Laure regularly meets one of her half-brothers, but prefers not to talk about it. It has not been possible for the family to be constituted: it does not exist.

When her second daughter reached the age of five, Marie-Laure broke with her mother definitively—now nearly fifteen years ago to the day. Marie-Laure finds it difficult to contain the emotion that is infused in everything she says. The psychosomatic conversation is often difficult, because the patient can be overwhelmed by the resurgence of painful memories, consequently raising what Freud calls the "quantum of mental excitations". I know from experience that patients suffering from severe illnesses are threatened by mental excitations that destabilise their entire psychosomatic system. Her memory of the break with her mother has certainly been painful to evoke, and I try to "turn the page" by addressing another problem, in order to introduce a transition to lessen her emotion, in a form of scansion. This is a conversation rather than psychotherapy, but sometimes the therapeutic dimension can manifest, as is so clear from Winnicott's cases; in fact, a single conversation can also have some beneficial aspects.

The break with her mother occurred in the same period in which she found her partner, who in this way played an important supporting role. I have wondered, until now, about the maternal relationship (presence of the internalised object) and Marie-Laure's life drive, but I have not yet wondered about the destiny of the aggressive drives: what does she do when she does not agree? What does she do in a case of conflict? My hypothesis is as follows: she has rejected her mother as a bad mother with whom she has broken; are we therefore dealing with a schizoparanoid core? Is there a "good-and-bad-mother" splitting; with her partner having played the role of the good mother, is the bad mother rejected? The psychotherapist, man or woman, can play the role of a "good mother"; we know that Freud was averse to playing such a role and that this is something for which he criticised Ferenczi.

As if in reply to my silent questions, Marie-Laure returns to the stressful conditions of her work and professional environment.

Female train drivers are in a minority and they live in a world of "macho" men.

I am now going to be able to assess her capacity to fulfil her aggressive impulses. This continual conscious and unconscious exchange between Marie-Laure and myself, moving back and forth between present and past, must be maintained in our relationship.

She complains about the violence towards the women of the men that she works with and wonders how long she will be able to tolerate this working environment, because, at the age of fifty-three, Marie-Laure has not built up enough annual contributions to be able to retire; the horizon of sixty years old still seems so far away. She tells me in this way about her worry for the future—how is she going to be able to bear all the years to come? She is experiencing some pain in the capsule of her right shoulder and epicondylitis, which has sometimes forced her to take time off that is poorly tolerated by her superiors, although it is carrying out her work that causes these pains.

In my classes at the medical faculty, I often tell my students that the question that must always be asked is: what role is the illness and physical pain playing in the psychosomatic equilibrium?

It seems that the physical pain is protecting her from attacks she has undergone at her workplace; I therefore have a preliminary answer about the destiny of the aggressive drives and their de-fusion from the life drives. Her aggressive drives seem to be turned against herself, but at the same time the motor physical problem constitutes a stage of somatic defence against more severe afflictions—the self-destruction is limited. I wonder whether the psychic apparatus and the mechanisms that inhibit the aggressive drives are being overwhelmed. I would like to draw attention here to the role played by somatic functions in bodily problems; the somatic functions belong to systems that constitute stages in psychosomatic disorganisation. When the stage of psychic defences is abandoned, the somatic defences carry out their roles of protecting the psychosomatic human entity.

We then leave the associative thread of the professional domain to consider her relationships. Marie-Laure has a couple of friends whom she meets when she stays in the mountains, but this happens rarely; it cannot be concluded that she has many friends. Moreover, as her elder daughter has left, only her younger child's presence at home provides her with some company.

I strongly emphasise my patient's isolation; she has mourned neither her marriage, nor her partner; nor has she ever resolved her relationship with a mother with whom she has broken. I wonder to myself about her capacity to live alone and to survive in the future. This is a question that I ask myself about every patient, every time I meet them.

We are reaching the end of the interview, and it is therefore important to prepare for separation so that the patient's level of mental excitation is as low as possible in order to get them through the day without any major emotional repercussions on her condition. This precaution is essential because a high level of unelaborated mental excitations can aggravate a somatic state; this is a heavy responsibility. As psychosomaticians, we have to be capable of separating from our patients because the end of every conversation can be considered as a mourning that therefore poses the risk of suffering for the patient. This is slightly less of a problem in the hospital setting, since the nurses can quickly take over emotionally; in Marie-Laure's case, we know that she has difficulties with mourning and separating from the other and from others.

She asks me how our conversation went and whether it was satisfactory. I reply to her—to advance her psychotherapy with her psychiatrist—that our entire conversation reveals the difficulties in her relationship with her mother, which must continue to be analysed so that she can gradually resolve this affective and conflictual problem from which she is suffering, which is demonstrated by all the separations of her last twenty years. I add that the therapeutic work that she has undertaken for her benefit is often accompanied by anxiety attacks and even depressive phases, and I encourage her to continue her efforts. We smile at each other and, as I leave her, I begin to reflect on the assessment of her psychosomatic risks.

Assessing the psychosomatic risk

Over the last nineteen years, since Pierre Marty's death, I have gradually developed a method of assessing psychosomatic risk (Appendix) in the course of my consultations at the hospital.

There are two stages to the psychosomatic interview: the first is a clinical interview with the patient to assess his mental and psychoaffective capacities in his family and professional environment, which allows hypotheses to be made about his capability to follow medical instructions, his capacity for personal fulfilment in family and professional life and leisure activities, and a context to be established for the patient's quality of life now and in the future. This is a difficult task that can take some time. We are helped in this work of mental elaboration by the knowledge of metapsychology acquired from Freud and developed throughout the twentieth century by the various schools of psychoanalysis and psychosomatics in France, North America, and Germany (c.f., Foreword).

The second stage is the consultation of the medical file kept by the doctors, which has to be read carefully, and only *after* the psychosomatic interview. Preliminary knowledge of the medical file creates the risk of disturbing the psychosomatician's perception whereas, in the interview, he must concentrate on listening to his patient. It is very important to hear the patient's account of his illness, rather than the doctors' account; these are two entirely different histories, and my medical colleagues would be surprised to hear the diagnoses "invented" by our patients or the "real" illnesses from which they suffer. Some patients have an encyclopaedic knowledge of all the symptoms described by the doctors, but this is a trap for the psychosomatician because this knowledge is often used for the purpose of defensive intellectualisation. Our patients can show an inexhaustible capacity to avoid talking about themselves by showing how much knowledge they have, as an attempt to show themselves in a positive light.

I therefore go to the room that holds all our medical files, and I begin to open Marie-Laure's file to study it. Does what she has told me correspond to the notes made in her file? What has she omitted to tell me, and why? We have to discover "lies by omission", and the reasons for them. This is ordinary work in psychoanalysis—verbal slips, parapraxes, compulsion to repeat behaviour, and so on—but it is also crucial in medicine, as these have to be interpreted in the doctor–patient relationship.

My patient is suffering from multiple metabolic syndrome and arterial hypertension with a major cardiovascular risk; her file records excessive diurnal somnolence, and her nocturnal sleep is interrupted by waking several times with a severe apnoea syndrome. She has been undergoing the menopause for two years. The arterial hypertension began when she was only twenty-eight years old, whereas the multiple metabolic syndrome is recent (slightly more than two years). She has been a heavy smoker in the past, stopping three years ago; she suffers from epicondylitis and tendinitis in her upper limbs—symptoms that are connected with her professional activity. The androgenically-distributed weight has been showing some improvement for a year, and the doctors attribute this excess weight to a problem in eating behaviour rather than any metabolic deficiency or a side-effect of any medication.

I will digress here slightly concerning metabolic syndrome (Giral & Cuzin, 2003; Hansel, 2007). Metabolic syndrome is diagnosed when three of the following criteria are met:

- a measurable increase in the waistline
- an increase in the arterial pressure (over 130/85mmHg)
- a fasting glycaemia higher than 1g/l
- an increase in triglycerides (over 1.5g/l)
- a reduction in "good" (HDL) cholesterol (less than 0.5g/l in men and 0.4g/l in women).

Abdominal obesity is indicated by an accumulation of visceral fat, which increases the risk of cardiovascular and metabolic disease. The doctor has to measure his patients' waistlines systematically: 102cm for men and 88cm for women. A waistline measuring over 88cm is found in 11.6 per cent of women aged forty-five to fifty years, 14.3 per cent of women aged fifty to fifty-five years, and 20.2 per cent of those aged over fifty-five years. This excess visceral adipose fat causes various abnormalities, such as type 2 diabetes, arterial hypertension, or dyslipidaemia. Epidemiological studies have shown an increase in the relative risk of cardiovascular mortality, myocardial infarction, and general mortality in patients with an enlarged waistline.

It is also important to know that even a slight reduction in weight brings a significant reduction in the risks associated with abdominal obesity. Dietary recommendations are important in this respect, and it is preferable to manage with a modest calorific reduction in conjunction with what I often recommend, which is a change in eating behaviour, rather than a diet that the patient would be content with following for a shorter or longer period.

I often tell my students and patients that weight loss can only be established over longer periods than those envisaged by my medical colleagues; I am thinking of three- to five-year periods necessary for losing five to ten kilos in order to consolidate, over ten years in total, an ideal weight adapted to the patient's new eating behaviours. The time that I indicate observes much more closely the body's adaptation to new ways of eating. Excessively fast weight loss constitutes an attack for the body, and the central nervous system, as the main agent that controls eating behaviours, not understanding what is suddenly happening, does everything it can to store what are assumed to be the necessary calories to ensure the survival of the body that it is controlling. The central nervous system precisely calculates weight based on current data; it is these data that have to be changed. According to my clinical experience, the central nervous system has very long periods of adaptation, and the weight loss has to be achieved in a similar way to going down a staircase stopping at each step. Observing such a procedure allows the brain to encode the weight reduction gradually and to maintain the weight that the patient wishes to reach. It is important to understand that this requires an alliance between the patient's ego and the central "management" organ of the body—the central nervous system (or CNS); knowing your body well is the best strategy. The benefits of physical exercise have been abundantly demonstrated, and must accompany the changes in eating behaviour.

Marie-Laure's psychosomatic risk

Marie-Laure has returned to some physical activity; she is being treated by a physiotherapist and the doctors emphasise that this is a patient with a good observance of medical advice.

How does a psychosomatician analyse the data presented above? We first have to ascertain the latency periods between life events and the emergence of somatic symptoms; the arterial hypertension that has become resistant over time emerged soon after her first daughter was born and, according to my hypothesis, was considerably reinforced by the conflict with her husband, which ended in a divorce three years after the symptom appeared, combined with continuous work-related stress over a twenty-year period. No doctor can overlook the consequences of life events on the general equilibrium; to these two events, we must add the patient's incapacity to mourn even her conflictual relationships. I must note here the existence of a masochistic component that enabled her to tolerate difficult situations for lengthy periods.[2]

Having reached the age of fifty, two years before I examined her, our patient became menopausal, which constitutes a challenge to be overcome; she has to adapt psychically to a new, altered state of her body.

This period is very often accompanied by depression, and my medical colleagues emphasise the patient's depressed state, for which her psychiatrist had prescribed an antidepressant. The menopause is often accompanied by changes in the body image that represent an ordeal for women. As will be seen later, in another case presentation relating to organ transplants, we are dealing with two changes: a change in the neuronal body image and a change in the psychic body image.

The patient also has difficulties adapting to changes in her life situations, especially in her body; she is deeply regressed and psychically fixed in an "oral" position, since oral satisfactions (food, cigarettes, etc.) are the favoured formulas of her equilibrium. The results are visible, since she has put on forty kilos in twenty years and her current body-mass index (BMI) is 31.5, that is to say obese (from 30 to 35). The patient's resources are limited, since physical activities are only recent and still very infrequent; there are no leisure activities, friendly relationships are restricted to rare annual meetings, and there is no love relationship. We note that the "zone" of satisfaction in life is very limited. This state can only cause us concern for the future, especially given that if the psychiatrist does not manage to instigate the mourning process, the patient will be in danger when she takes her retirement, and, of course, when her second daughter leaves home. The future looks bleak if we follow a scenario of the patient's progressive disorganisation caused by her retirement and the incapacity to redeploy her energy in projects that might support the life drives. My report on the consultation could therefore contain some pessimistic comments.

But we can also envisage a second scenario by considering the following positive elements: presence of a narcissistic core (self-love) that allows the patient to continue to take care of herself, as shown by her physical appearance at the time of the consultation; the presence of a masochistic core that enables her to tolerate painful ordeals; and finally the presence of a capacity to observe medical guidance. This is a crucial factor in medicine and psychosomatics, because the doctors know (and there are statistics to prove it) that the proportion of patients following medical recommendations is increasingly low, hence the questions often raised about the efficacy of medicine. A patient who follows the prescriptions is therefore favourably viewed by the medical staff, who form the hypothesis that the somatic risk is consequently lower.

Another factor in the patient's favour is the relationship of trust that she maintains with "good mother figures"; this relationship with external objects, such as the nurses, doctors, psychosomaticians, and so on enables her to lead her life. The nurses have noted this behaviour, as they have written in their logbook: "good observance, the stay in hospital has restored her spirits a little". I often tell my students that, for some patients, *the hospital is a good mother*, and that is borne out in Marie-Laure's case. The nurses' logbook should never be overlooked when considering patients.

The importance of a favourable environment that is conducive to improving health can therefore be noted; my therapeutic recommendations will be made according to the hypothesis of a favourable environment. If, in her psychotherapy, Marie-Laure manages to strengthen her capacities to invest her vital energy in new activities, such as friends, leisure pastimes, and physical activities, we can then take a more optimistic view of her future at a seven-year horizon. We cannot predict the accidents of life, but if the therapy does not achieve its objective—if Marie-Laure cannot confront the separation from her daughter and her work when she retires—we will be confronted with a severe problem of probable somatic disorganisations: cardiovascular risk and arterial hypertension.

Where the medical and psychosomatic predictions converge and diverge

The current medical approach is essentially based on analysing the biological factors and the patient's medical history; the integrative psychosomatic examination, as I have developed it, considers the state of psychic functioning and its relation to somatic and psychic incidents in the patient's history. To this, I add the effect of the malfunctioning of the mental apparatus on the neurological and entire biological system. This approach concerns all somatic pathologies, and in this respect I agree with my friend and colleague Christophe Dejours's observation that there are no psychosomatic illnesses or psychosomatic patients.

I am putting forward the hypothesis that the psychic apparatus participates to a greater or lesser degree in all somatic pathologies. If we take the medical approach, we note that Marie-Laure is in serious danger of cardiovascular risk in the long-term; if we add the psychosomatic analysis we can understand that the cardiovascular risk can be greatly reduced by reintroducing Marie-Laure's capacity to change her behaviour. Adding in the psychosomatic analysis means that we are reintroducing the dimension of the subject to medical practice.

The stability of psychic functioning is initially assessed on the basis of a person's relationship with his first love object—the mother, or maternal substitute. All research in psychoanalysis and the neurosciences emphasises the importance, in the first case, of psychic programming, and in the second, of neuronal programming in the earliest years of life. For human beings, and mammals in general, these two forms of programming occur through the relationship to the mother, who herself exists in a relationship to the father, who is himself integrated into a wider environment. Psychoanalysts refer to the "introjection of the object", confirming that the first stage of human psychosexual development has been completed (for Klein, at around nine months, in the ninth-month depression that signals this internalisation).

The unconscious perception of my relationship with Marie-Laure evolved throughout the interview; sitting opposite me was a woman of about fifty years, who seemed to want to talk. Then, her constant quest for approval led me to wonder about the new image that she was communicating to me; the pathological mournings gradually returned to what Klein terms the ninth-month depression, indicating that the child has introjected the maternal object, making him capable of coping with the mother's absence. The object seemed to me to be unstable; I perceived a fragile being in distress, and I still sensed in her the emotion connected with this demand for presence. The breakdown of the relationship with her mother led me to consider the hypothesis that, although she had separated from her mother, she had developed a strategy for moving as close as possible to her "good object" choices and protecting herself against the "bad object" by separations (e.g., from her mother) or from her managers at work by means of somatic problems. She was therefore in the position of splitting the good and the bad object: her mother was the bad object that she kept at a distance in time, and the doctors, medical staff, her husband, daughters, and so on were good objects with whom she could maintain relations because they allowed her to reduce the mental excitations connected with the stress of her life. I suppose that her superiors belonged to the bad objects. At the end of the interview, the image I had deep inside of me was of a fragile little girl who had been left on her own. One really wanted to help her, and the nurses were right about this in their comments.

On the theoretical level of integrative psychosomatics it can be noted that the psychic apparatus has not been able to provide an equilibrium to the patient at a very early stage, and that, through her oral libidinal fixations, the hypothalamic component[3] of the central nervous system has provided the general equilibrium in conjunction with the psyche. We are confronted with interrelations between two systems that can provide a state of equilibrium in the psychosomatic unity; this is what I called the dual-control model, before establishing the model of the five systems.

The psychosomatic clinical examination form

Once the clinical examination has been conducted, it is advisable to complete the form (below) that I have developed from a new grid of the characteristics of somatic patients' functioning and a new nosography; this document considerably facilitates the communication between doctors and psychosomaticians, and enables us to assess the patient's psychosomatic risk.

Concerning the creation and scientific development of this methodological tool, entitled: "Method for assessing and diagnosing psychosomatic health; the general assessment of psychosomatic risk", I have written the following brief introduction.

This psychosomatic diagnostic tool was developed from my research into professional stress undertaken from 1980; this has been the subject of many publications in France and worldwide, in particular with Prof Cary Cooper of Manchester University and with a group of researchers from twenty-four countries. In 1984, I joined Pierre Marty at the Institute of Psychosomatics, which he founded in 1978, and I undertook some research with him from 1987 on the psychosomatic classification that he had developed. I published some of our research findings jointly with him, and after his death I continued to apply this classification, leading to two publications in psychiatric journals (Stora, 1994, 1995).

Applying this classification led me to conclude that the Marty classification was incomplete and could not be used in its current form by doctors and psychologists if it was to be turned into a tool of psychosomatic diagnosis and a method of epidemiological research. Pierre Marty possessed considerable clinical experience that he had not yet integrated into his classification.

I used many North American classifications for my research, and finally I formulated the present-day method, of which I have used a first outline to assess the greater or lesser risk of rejection in heart transplant patients. My publication now forms a chapter of the book on cardiology published by the heart transplant department at La Pitié-Salpêtrière (Gandjbakhch et al., 2000).

This method makes it possible to form a diagnosis and a strategy for psychotherapeutic treatment, as well as epidemiological studies in integrative psychosomatics. It is over a year ago that I undertook an investigation into breast cancer with Dr Pascale Surugue and colleagues from the Institut Curie, with a view to validating the method that I have developed.

I know that psychoanalysts are opposed to such investigations, but, in Pierre Marty's lifetime and subsequently, our publications have proved that it is possible. Epidemiological research does not have therapeutic objectives, but sets out to compare structures of psychic and psychosomatic functioning in a way that allows patients' points of vulnerability to be ascertained in order to assess their psychosomatic functioning and consequently their risk factors in psychic and somatic dimensions. I introduced the concept of risk to meet the concerns of the doctors with whom I work at La Pitié-Salpêtrière.

Every observed patient (anamnesis) must first be resituated in the three dimensions to which the human being belongs, according to the bio-psycho-social model developed in Boston by Professor Engel.

I also refer to:

1. The model of the psychic apparatus in Freud's metapsychology, and his first and second topography, articulated according to Marty's theoretical proposition from the integration of the second phase of the anal stage. I also adopt Freud's theory of the drives, emphasising the process of fusion and de-fusion (I particularly emphasise the second theory of the drives, life drives, death drives).
2. For a more detailed study of the stages of pregenital development, the models of Klein, Meltzer, Winnicott, Bion, Joyce McDougall, E. Kestenberg.
3. For narcissism, mainly Kohut's contributions (the grandiose self and Ego Ideal), as well as Grunberger and Green.
4. For masochism, Freud's contributions and, more recently, Rosenberg's important work.

As an example, here is the form for Marie-Laure.

RESULTS OF THE PSYCHOSOMATIC CLINICAL EXAMINATION
JBS-PSYSOMA–21 October 2010 version THE PSYCHOSOMATIC GRID
Developed by J. B. STORA from 1993 to 2011.

Surname   [Omitted]
Forename   Marie-Laure
Date of birth Fifty-three years old

THE CLINICAL EXAMINATION CONSIDERS THE FOUR DIMENSIONS OF THE FUNCTIONING OF THE PSYCHOSOMATIC UNITY PSYCHIC PROCESSES AND MECHANISMS, CHARACTEROLOGICAL AND BEHAVIOURAL MANIFESTATIONS, SUBLIMATORY ACTIVITIES ETC. PREVALENCE OF BEHAVIOURS CAPACITY FOR EXPRESSING AFFECTS RISK ASSOCIATED WITH THE FAMILY AND PROFESSIONAL ENVIRONMENT.		NOTE
PSYCHIC PROCESSES AND MECHANISMS:	Axis 1A: object relationship: 1- presence of the object 2- assessment of the narcissistic dimension (presence of grandiose Self, Ego Ideal) 3- assessment of the masochistic dimension 4- assessment of the density of the preconscious (imaginative capacity, associations, dreams) Axis 1B: psychic states and events in personal life: anxieties, mournings, depressions, traumas, cultural influences Axis 1C: somatic fixations, psychic fixations Axis 1D: defence mechanisms Axis 1E: presence of certain character traits: phobic, hysterical, perverse; predominantly oral, predominantly anal, phallic-narcissistic, sado-masochistic relationship Axis 1F: sublimatory activities	RESULT
	***	

(*Continued*)

	1. Balanced psychic functioning: capacity to remember the past, capacity to move back and forth between present and past, capacity for elaboration. **2. Temporarily impaired psychic functioning: abnormalities of mental functioning-possibilities of mental elaboration temporarily overwhelmed by excessive excitations or a suppression of representations.** 3. Deeply impaired psychic functioning: operative life and thinking. 4. Severely impaired psychic functioning: progressive disorganisations—essential depression.	2
2. Prevalence of behaviours	1. Controlled and integrated behaviour. 2. Low prevalence 3. Medium. 4. Strong.	3
3. Capacity for expressing affects	1. Well-integrated representations and affects, 2. Suppression with three possible outcomes (displacement, e.g., phobia, obsessions; unconnected with the representation: e.g., hysteria, transformation, anxiety neurosis), 3. Predominance of affects of vitality in the relationship, 4. Affects representing the memory of a traumatic unrepresentable experience, 5. Alexithymia.	2
4. Risk connected with the environment	Nature of the environment. Family environment and professional environment. The examination assesses the adaptational capacities used and/or the possible detriment to psychosomatic health (traumas). 1. Very satisfactory level, 2. Satisfactory, 3. Temporary minor impairment,	4

(*Continued*)

| | 4. Medium-level difficulties,
5. Substantial impairment,
6. Major impairment leading to a temporary functional incapacity,
7. Long-term incapacity for autonomous functioning. | |

DIAGNOSIS ACCORDING TO THE PSYCHOSOMATIC NOSOGRAPHY ESTABLISHED BY J. B. Stora:
Character neurosis (according to Marty's nosography: neurosis with uncertain mentalisation).
Assessment of psychosomatic risk
Absence of risk: stable
Short-term impact: 5
Low to moderate risk: 5 to 10
Moderate to high risk: 10 to 15—possibility of reversibility, reorganisation based on fixation–regression points, monitoring, instability.
High to very high risk: 15 or higher (general instability of the disorganised psychosomatic unity).

Axis 5. Assessment of somatic risk.	
5 levels: Very high risk High risk Medium risk Low risk No risk	Based on the results of observation, and the diagnoses and prognoses communicated by the patient's doctors. **3 medium risk**
General assessment of psychosomatic functioning:	
Comparing the psychic risk with the somatic risk to reach a general assessment. * Subject at high risk– general instability of the disorganised psychosomatic unity.	You must compare the psychic risk (table below to be completed) and the somatic risk subsequently communicated by the doctors to obtain the evaluation of the general psychosomatic risk. Evaluate convergence and divergence of the two risks, which are dynamically interrelated, according to the theory of systems (J. B. Stora).

* Subject at medium risk—possibility of reversibility of the symptoms, reorganisation from fixation-points. Monitoring the possible instability. * Subject at low risk, high potential of reorganisation. * Stable subject whose psychic apparatus is overwhelmed, short-term impact.	**General risk: 14** The patient's psychotherapeutic treatment should enable her ultimately to strengthen her personality and acquire the capacity to live alone and to cathect her energy in various activities, as well as to form satisfactory object relationships. Where these therapeutic objectives are not met, there is a risk that the patient's health will deteriorate severely in the long term.

You must give your conclusions above (diagnostic and prognostic); for example, extreme vulnerability, difficulties observing the treatments, recommendation of psychotherapeutic treatment, and so on.

The doctors need to have some conclusions so as to understand their patients' development better.

Signature of the psychosomatician psychotherapist.

To know more about the method of evaluating psychosomatic risk (J. B. Stora), see: www.psychosomatique-integrative.net

CHAPTER TWO

Chloé: repairing the psychic apparatus—neuronal tumour, neuropsychoanalysis, or neuropsychosomatics?

In my integrative psychosomatics practice at La Pitié-Salpêtrière, I see patients from every hospital department. I will now present the case of a young woman who contacted me following an operation for a glioma in her brain. What follows concerns the progression of a psychosomatic psychotherapy over nearly two years, by which I was severely tested as a psychotherapist.

Once patients have been operated on, what happens to them?

Unlike classical psychoanalysis, in psychosomatics the patient and the therapist sit facing each other. I will indicate some other forms of this particular psychotherapy as I explain the therapeutic process here.

First meeting: the memory of words[1]

Chloé phoned me to make an appointment, with a view to conducting a psychoanalysis. She contacted me following a recommendation from my colleague, the neurosurgeon who had operated on her. She had obtained some information about me by consulting some websites, and had read one of my books. I asked her first about her current condition—she replied that she had recently had an operation for a glioma, a brain tumour in the prefrontal cortices. She worked in a large library in the capital, and we arranged an appointment for October.

Chloé is a slender woman, around 175cm tall with dark brown hair, who fixes me with a stare that I initially think is questioning, but then suddenly strikes me as vacant during the session. This sensation of looking at someone whose gaze has disappeared can be disturbing for the psychotherapist—what has disappeared from her personality since the surgery?

Following her operation five months earlier, Chloé had suffered from some phonemic paraphasias, as well as epileptic fits that occurred in the evening every two to three weeks; she also has long periods of insomnia. Phonological paraphasias are very common manifestations of aphasia and have often been described in the literature. They are a qualitative problem of oral expression that affects lexical production in an aphasic syndrome. This issue is characterised by a verbal production that does not correspond to the words the speaker wants to use, and derives from a phonological similarity with the target. These mistakes are also involuntary. Three aphasic syndromes are generally described as the most liable to produce phonological paraphasias: Broca's aphasia, Wernicke's aphasia, predominantly phonemic, and conduction aphasia.

During the first few minutes of our interview, we reviewed the incidents connected with the consequences of her paraphasias; Chloé's speech has a foreign inflection that is a mixture of English and German—she tells me that this dates back to her operation. When I ask about her knowledge of languages, she tells me that she studied English and German, both of which she still speaks. The interview takes a chaotic course, with many silences and hesitations—she seems to be searching for her words, because if I do not ask a question or keep the conversation going, Chloé looks at me without replying. I realise that I must maintain the verbal connection, because what seems to have been damaged in the neurosurgical operation is the capacity for understanding long spoken sentences; her capacities have been gradually returning with the help of a speech therapist who has been treating her since her surgery. Chloé does not remember what is said; I adapt quickly and address her using short sentences. I come to the conclusion that these are mild paraphasic problems.

I silently make a note to myself to meet the neurosurgeon after one or two sessions with Chloé, in order to assess the operation and its neurological consequences. It is important that a psychosomatician should obtain information about his patient's medical records. I make a mental note that it is not only the intonation of words, but also access to her verbal memory, as well as her working memory, that seem to have been impaired.

Every time I say nothing there is another silence, and when I ask her, "What are you thinking about?" she replies, "nothing". Unlike the many neurotic patients in whom we quickly detect the mechanism of repression, I observe that Chloé is really not thinking about anything; there is a blank in thought, and we are dealing with a mental emptiness that has neurological rather than psychic origins.

I soon realise that I must gradually build with her, in the therapeutic relationship, the links between words, emotions, and thoughts—both her current and her past thoughts. We must work on recovering the semantic memory and the mental and affective representations of her past. This in an objective of therapeutic work that I must confirm after my interview with her neurosurgeon. The processes relating to psychic connections seem to have been damaged by the disappearance of some of the networks of neuronal connections.

Several times during the session, Chloé showed emotions that I sensed strongly in her infraverbal and unconscious communication. So that she could gradually understand the nature of the therapeutic relationship and the work that we would be doing together, I told her what I was sensing—namely some helplessness—which she confirmed to me. This was an emotion connected with her condition and her incapacity to mobilise quickly the rich vocabulary to which she had previously been accustomed—a feeling of being paralysed. She was really in distress.

To be able to work therapeutically, since Chloé was unable to mobilise her thought to converse with me, I decided on the following therapeutic strategy: to start asking her questions gradually, addressing all the possible associative chains (by semantic fields): her vocation as a librarian, her curiosity about books, her university studies, her current work, her family, her friends, and so on; in short, to begin to reactivate, build, and strengthen a network of associative chains (thereby also reinforcing the synaptic connections). Hanna Damasio and her colleagues at the University of Iowa have demonstrated that tasks in which subjects have to name people, animals, or tools activate different regions of the temporal cortex. This helps to explain why lesions that only affect a relatively small area of the temporal lobe sometimes entail the loss of words that refer to a category of particular objects. Ojemann's research in electrophysiology has shown that language is organised by semantic categories rather than words. The therapeutic strategy that I have used corresponds to the above-mentioned neuroscientific works (Purves et al., 2004, p. 599).

She read books, possibly fairy tales, when she was very young; these books were close at hand on a small shelf beside her desk in her classroom at school. She opened and read them enthusiastically, and so she always got zero in her dictation (emergence of humour—self-irony), which we laughed about together. Her mother also brought her books to read from the library at the secondary school where she taught.

She naturally goes on to talk about her mother, and I sense deeply the hostility she feels towards her and point this out to her. She agrees with this and tells me that her mother has always shown aggression towards her and her two sisters; in her opinion, she has a psychiatric condition. I remain pensive; she adds that she cannot indicate to me any kind of diagnosis. I answer that it may be a question of character traits that have been interpreted as psychiatric problems; she then adds that her mother was also committed but she does not know the reasons why.

When she was seventeen years old, she left her family to go to Paris and pursue studies initially in literature, and then in librarianship. She is now thirty-eight years old and lives with a young man, André, who is also a colleague. When she talks about André, I feel a certain hostility in her voice, with an intensity that is akin to her relationship with her mother. She is hostile towards him because he has helped her throughout recent months, and in a way this has made her annoyed with him. This shows her narcissistic dimension: "I can solve this on my own." She keeps anyone who wants to help her at a distance. I question what effect this will have in the therapeutic relationship, and make a note of this observation.

She is having difficulties with André, and cannot see what her immediate and future destiny in the library will be; how is she going to be able to manage when dealing with all her colleagues? While she does not look handicapped, she is trying, as I note during our meetings, very slowly to recover her previous mental and verbal capacities. I tell her about my clinical experience with patients; it takes between nine and eighteen months for new synaptic connections to develop. She confirms to me that the neuropsychologist and the speech therapist have given her a horizon of around two years. She tells me just before the end of one of our meetings that she will be having chemotherapy in three months' time and that she may become dependent on social services. She does not communicate to me any anxious emotions connected with her anticipation of the treatment.

She had not paid me at the end of the first session, although I had suggested a much lower fee than is usual for a psychotherapist; we had made a further appointment and I preferred to be patient because I did not actually know very many facts about her life and, above all, her psychic functioning following the operation. Chloé needed help, and the payment did not seem important to me.

In our relationship, Chloé sometimes appeared to me very robotic, while at times also very human in her desire to recover her verbal capacities, which led me to wonder: how can we help a human being to recover his portion of humanity? In this respect I am thinking of the painstaking therapeutic work of my neuropsychologist colleagues, who deal with brain-damaged patients all day long. The lack of emotional tone in Chloé's language makes me wonder, and I think about the normal tonal emotional components, described as prosodic elements, which give additional meaning to verbal communication. These deficiencies, which are called aprosodies, are associated with lesions in the cortical regions of the right hemisphere, which correspond to Broca and Wernicke regions in the left hemisphere. However, I form the hypothesis that, in Chloé's case, the absence of affect has a psychic origin.

I continue to explore the neuronal and psychic deficiencies caused by the operation: Chloé explains to me that when she reads a book (since I was asking her what books she had recently read), she remembers the atmosphere and the climate of the book, but not the characters and what they say to each other. This confirms that the right hemisphere is functioning well. I will return to her difficulties later on in this chapter.

From our early meetings, I remember the conflictual relationship with her mother, an absent father, dominated by the mother, and a disunited parental couple. She also has a younger sister, who, at the time of Chloé's operation, broke away violently from her family by leaving them to live with her child on a boat in a port in Brittany. She had not yet spoken to me about her younger sister, but this relationship seemed important.

I leave Chloé with many questions in my mind, because it seems that by not paying me, she has managed to create a conflictual situation that replicates her relationship with her mother; I think this repetition of a psychodynamic situation is a favourable sign in regards to the prognosis of her psychotherapy.

Meeting: continuing with the anamnesis

Chloé gives me a different impression today, and we talk in a friendly and empathetic way from the beginning of the session. She tells me that she had been very tired in the previous session—I must recognise that it was the same for me, but I do not tell her this. Her tiredness is often caused by her nocturnal epileptic fits; she had had an epileptic fit the previous Saturday, and therefore had felt very tired in our session on the Monday. We continue the session by addressing, according to my therapeutic choice, a great many problems in her daily life and in her past. I also ask her about her dreams in order to ascertain more about the quality of her mental life; she tells me that she has not had any dreams since last year, but that before then her dreams were filled with anxiety. She remembered from her previous dreams some disturbing images of her teeth being rotten and falling out. We have not yet done any associative work on her dreams, but I think these date from the period before the glioma was discovered and the manifestations of alarm in the somatic body.

It all began one year earlier; she collapsed after an epileptic fit that resulted in a coma. She returned to work three months later, and her glioma was operated on at the end of the first quarter of the following year.

She talks again about her younger sister, Catherine, who has a boat on which she is currently living with her young daughter. She recently quarrelled with Catherine, because Catherine compared the destinies of the three daughters in the family; for Catherine, the three sisters have had an identical destiny, coloured by their mother's violence. Chloé does not have the same experience, and disagrees with Catherine's opinion because she thinks that she has suffered more than her two sisters have from their mother's violence. She explains to me that Catherine is a naval engineer and that she can easily gain access to boats. Catherine, who is going through a crisis with a family break-up, has written at great length (via e-mail) to many members of the extended family to reveal that their mother had been extremely violent towards her and her sisters throughout their childhood and adolescence. Since sending these emails, Catherine has been feeling uneasy and wishes to take back what she has done. Meanwhile Chloé's father has got back in touch—for Chloé, her father is "a stranger with odd behaviour", always distant, but nice. He apologised to her for having been silent for many years. He also apologised to Catherine and Sylvie, the youngest sister. There is a three-year gap between Sylvie and Chloé; Sylvie is an engineer, married, and the mother of a family. During the session, she likens her father's attitude to that of the French during the war, who watched trains going past, full of Jews being deported. This comment surprises me—why such an association? Chloé is not Jewish, but she reveals at this point her commitment to anarchism, united behind people "of no fixed abode" and all the causes that deserve her attention as a campaigner. Her opposition to her mother has been translated by this political engagement; she takes issue with society in its very foundations.

Chloé begins to reflect on her current situation and wonders why she has taken so many years to reflect on the dramatic problems in her life. I tell her that it is often after the age of thirty, or following a physical illness, that people start to reflect on their destiny, going back over their past to give meaning to their lives.

Since meeting her boyfriend, André, in the town where her parents live, he recently pointed out to her that she spoke to him harshly. Chloé tells me that she has never noticed this and that, for our "relationship", we do not know each other well enough for her to attack me. She has therefore integrated, from her early childhood, the violent atmosphere in which she has lived and grown up. Brain tumours are sometimes accompanied by a manifestation of aggressive impulses; instead, Chloé's words reveal, through her parental conflicts, the masochistic dimension of her personality: her mother used to beat her.

This helps to explain her escape into drugs. From as early as twelve years old, she began to smoke marijuana and drink alcohol with one of her girl-friends, and this continued until she met André. She gave up alcohol at the age of twenty-four, and continued to smoke marijuana occasionally; she also smokes cigarettes in large quantities.

I wonder very much how it will be possible to discover what effect this addiction has had on her capacity for concentration and attention, as well as on her mnemic capacities.

As if in response to my unconscious musings, Chloé tells me that, since the operation, her memory has been more auditory and no longer visual. She remembers what she hears, but in a limited way, and she does not remember what she reads in books; she makes notes and, once she has read them, she no longer knows which part of the book she has made them in. She cannot watch a film because she does not understand the dialogue between the characters; she also finds it difficult to follow their actions. She has brought me a book about the brain (Doidge, 2007), and asks me to read all the passages that she has underlined. This has taken considerable effort on her part.

She goes back over her past as a young girl and tells me that, as children, she and her sister Catherine were very gifted, achieving exceptionally high marks at school, until the baccalaureate; it is also true that many subjects did not interest them. By contrast, it was not the same with Sylvie, who was subjected to fierce attacks from her mother, who required her to have excellent marks like her two elder sisters.

We end the session, which I think has been excellent, by discussing the payment for the first of our sessions. She tells me that a friend had told her that no fee was charged for the first session with a psychoanalyst. I then adhere to the usual analytic practice to avoid unsettling her; these are sixty-minute psychosomatic psychotherapy sessions rather than a traditional psychoanalytic treatment.[2] I prefer to continue our work rather than disturb it with problems of technique and therapeutic strategy; one day, perhaps it will be possible to explain all this, or perhaps never. She pays me by writing a cheque, and I observe that she writes this without making any mistakes with either the amount or the date, which demonstrates that her motor capacities and access to the memory of written words are only slightly impaired.

Meeting with the neurosurgeon

My colleague from the neurosurgery department greets me warmly and kindly. He keeps me informed about every detail of the operation and devotes a lot of time to showing me all the surgical actions carried out on his computer screen.

The tumour was extensively visible on the surface and a location by stimulation was carried out once the patient had been wakened; the brain lesion had been revealed by epileptic fits that had been developing since six months before the operation. The location by stimulation triggered some partial fits that were quickly stopped by iced serum; these affected the control of bodily movements: elbow-fist-hand flexing, fist-hand flexing, jaw movements, and so on. My colleague indicates some phonemic paraphasias; the excision of the tumour was carried out while taking account, according to the places, of some phonemic or semantic paraphasias. He approached the motor paths without touching them, so as to avoid compounding the linguistic deficiency with a motor deficiency. After this brief account, I continue my search in the medical literature to deepen my knowledge.

This is a grade II glioma; the World Health Organization (WHO) classification revised in 2007 is not straightforward to reproduce because it does not take into account the heterogeneity of tumours and makes no distinction between tumorous cells and infiltrated residual parenchyma. The French Sainte-Anne classification has a better predictability, because it integrates clinical data and imagery by taking account of the results of the MRI investigation, which reveals the signs of necrosis and neo-vascularisation that are specific to high-grade tumours, but that does not apply in this case. Grade II tumours are called oligodendroglial tumours; this is an oligoastrocytoma, which is a mixed tumour combining the characteristics of astrocytomas and oligodendrogliomas. At La Pitié-Salpêtrière, the INSERM teams, led by Jean-Yves Delattre and Denis Delattre at the Institut Curie, have identified several types of deletion on chromosome one that are related to good prognosis for some gliomas. As it is difficult to establish a correct grading in the classification of gliomas, since it is essentially based on fine microscopic characteristics, I have preferred to omit them, for the time being, when predicting the psychosomatic risk in the development of this type of glioma.

In Chloé's case, the intervention was followed by severe aphasic problems that have since disappeared; the neurosurgeon also notes the relatively faint Germanic intonation. As mentioned above, Chloe is receiving treatment from a speech therapist.

Research into low-grade gliomas and brain plasticity gives me great hope for my patient's treatment; the dogma of Broca's localising model has been challenged. For some years, new data from surgery have been demonstrating, increasingly clearly, that massive cerebral excisions can be completely compensated for, without leaving any discernible functional deficiency. Pre- and post-surgical imaging techniques, as well as peri-operative stimulation procedures, make it possible to follow the nature and kinetics of these compensations. In fact, well before the surgical operation, and in response to the tumorous invasion, the process of synaptogenesis (formation of synapses between neurons) begins before the surgery and is consolidated after the operative procedure.

In the therapeutic strategy for Chloé, I have therefore taken into consideration the post-lesional brain plasticity that allows the nervous system to be reorganised following physical damage.

How psychosomatic psychotherapy can facilitate and aid the development of neuronal connections was the problem that confronted me; I was relying heavily on the plasticity of Chloé's brain to make progress.

The neuronal problems experienced by Chloé

In psychosomatics, we have developed two approaches to illness: the illness seen by the doctor (hence my meeting with the neurosurgeon) and the illness experienced by the patient. We also ask ourselves what role the illness is playing in the patient's psychosomatic equilibrium.

What was Chloé suffering from after the operation on her brain?

After her operation, Chloé suffered from paraphasia, epileptic fits, and long periods of insomnia. Her verbal memory and her memory of current experience were affected. She experienced emotions and feelings of distress connected mainly with her condition and her lack of vocabulary. As I emphasised above, sometimes she seemed to me very robotic, and sometimes very human, in her desire to recover her verbal capacities. She could remember the atmosphere and general feeling of books, but not the characters or their dialogue.

She was very tired in the first few sessions, often due to nocturnal epileptic fits. She had not dreamt since the previous year; before her operation she had many anxiety-related dreams. According to my clinical psychosomatic experience, these dreams are produced by the body sending warning signals to the psyche: the body senses that its homeostasis is at risk and the brain worries. Since the operation, her verbal memory has been auditory rather than visual. She remembers everything she hears well but not what she reads in books; she makes notes and having read them she no longer remembers where in the book she has made them.[3] She can no longer watch films either because she does not understand all the words she hears or she cannot follow the action of the characters (problem of integration in the auditory cortex). Chloé also wonders about her symptoms and, to help me understand her case, she brings me (see above) a neuropsychology book in which she has noted some paragraphs that I will quote below.

Concerning Alexandre Luria's famous patient, "the man with a shattered world", who is called Zazetsky, the book states:

> He could no longer understand logic, cause and effect, or spatial relationships. He couldn't distinguish his left from his right …. He couldn't comprehend a whole word, understand a whole sentence, or recall a complete memory because doing any of those things would require relating symbols. He could grasp only fleeting fragments. (Doidge, 2007, p. 33)

Chloé's operation has caused her some problems in her capacity to understand words, to put them together, to form them into intelligible sentences and to remember them all together.

She also tells me about the loss of her automatic linguistic functioning: when she talks with readers at the library, she does not remember all the questions they ask her; she only remembers the first question and tries to answer it. Automatic linguistic functioning, as with hello, goodbye, Happy New Year, and so on, seems to have disappeared. She cannot summon these expressions quickly; she has to think about it to know what she must say. She knows what all the words mean but cannot use them in a conversation. She likes punk music, but for now music is a noise that she cannot interpret; musical harmony has disappeared.

I set myself the following objectives based on our first few conversations and my knowledge of the state of her central nervous system after the operation.

How to bring Chloé back to life?

It would be necessary to:

- develop her capacity to form longer sentences, as she could only speak in short phrases expressing a single idea;
- develop her working memory and recall memory;
- recover her reading memory by means of motor (procedural) memory—this is a complex process that I will explain in the context of the progression of our encounters;
- develop her ability to listen to her body to prevent epileptic fits;
- facilitate her access to associations of ideas, to the preconscious, and to the elaborative capacity by making connections between different semantic fields, the associated emotions and feelings, and the recollection of behaviours.

In short, I needed to rebuild, with Chloé, a psychic apparatus that had been damaged by the tumour and the operation, and thereby to facilitate rebuilding and strengthening of the synaptic connections.

The concept of the psychic apparatus is totally alien to conventional medicine, and I must say that I make a great deal of effort with my colleagues so that they may understand its functioning and, above all, its existence.

I was unable to put together a team to care for my patient, with each specialist working separately, but Chloé provided the liaison and often informed the neurosurgeon about the progression of her therapeutic work; it is clear that the speech therapist's work was also outstanding.

Our meetings and our work continue

Chloé comes to the next session, bringing me a dream:

> *She is lying in her bed in her room and a woman is standing there lifting up the duvet; she shows her a cardboard box that contains a row of five children's bodies of different sizes.*

In the previous session, Chloé had brought me a huge number of drawings that she had done in the last fifteen years; we had discussed her artwork at length and I had encouraged her to return to this so that her right hand that suffered from the operation could function again as a result of this learning. I had also advised her to talk openly with Guillaume (her closest colleague) about the disturbances to her work caused by her operation; this colleague had noticed Chloé's handicap but did not dare to talk to her about it.

I began by drawing her attention to the five children's bodies, putting forward the hypothesis that they probably represented her hand, with its five fingers. Chloé cannot associate for the time being, but she has gradually understood how a dream is interpreted. The use of metaphors in this case helps her to understand that the hand's five fingers were enclosed in a cardboard box. She then thinks (this is her interpretation) that it would be difficult for now to return to drawing; hence the five unusable fingers lined up in a cardboard box. This is a possible interpretation that I accept; she states that she is tired and cannot go back to drawing.

She has begun to talk with Guillaume and André, who understand her fatigue much better and her difficulty working at the library. She talks to me at length about her relationship with the readers because I ask her about this; she recognises that, because of her current difficulties, some people think she is stupid. She finds this hurtful (a narcissistic injury), but says nothing.

I must say that the consequences of her operation meant that Chloé could appear like someone with whom it is difficult to communicate and who does not always understand what is being said to her.

The operation has caused problems in her capacity to understand words, to put them together, to form intelligible sentences from them and to remember them all together. When I talk to her using short sentences she understands perfectly, and we can have long conversations for nearly an hour about many subjects, such as Buñuel's films, Bergman, and the American series or books she has been able to read. She recognises that, with time, she is beginning to recover some of her capacities for attention and concentration, but these have not yet been completely acquired.

Her eyes often get tired and this prevents her from devoting time to reading. She cannot focus her attention and remember what she reads (slight deficiency of the short-term memory). This is therefore an auditory impairment at a very high level of cortical integration, which affects assembling words (the heard word and the read word). Nevertheless, there are some semantic capacities and it seems that she can recover them by working with the speech therapist, and with an orthoptist whom she is also consulting.

In the sessions I am trying to inject some imagination and auditory capacities by the use of metaphors, which is ordinary therapeutic work in psychosomatics. Pierre Marty called this "lending your apparatus for dealing with thoughts". At the end of the session, Chloé is still tired; she smiles at me kindly and states that she had been tired when she arrived and that now the session has restored her will to live; we then part.

Next meeting: the "mirror function" emerges

When she arrives at the session, Chloé sits down timidly on the edge of the armchair and looks at me questioningly, anticipating everything from me. She looks at me as a child looks at her mother who is going to take the initiative of speaking to her, telling her things about life, making her feel emotions, and so on. The psychotherapist's maternal function is primordial in psychosomatics. For her, I must be the mirror[4] of her thoughts and of the experience of her thoughts so that she can rebuild herself.

I begin by asking her about the meeting that week with the neuropsychologist, who made her take a test and told her that it is her working memory that is functioning poorly. Of course, Chloé and I realised this some time ago now, but this explanation does not satisfy me; I must find a technical procedure that she could use for training so as to recover some of her capacity for understanding long and abstract sentences. As explained above, Chloé does not understand the combination of words in a sentence that is too long.

Before a technical procedure can be formulated, Chloé and I talk about her relationship with André and Guillaume and with her work, as well as her relationship with the readers. She is still in the same situation because they are not patient, and often she cannot remember the subjects of the books they choose. She is hurt by the way they look at her. She thinks that she is no longer suited to the quick work of selecting and accessing books, and feels lost and misunderstood. Chloé is reliving some past episodes of narcissistic wounds and difficulties in overcoming conflictual situations.

We move on, by association, to physical exercises and sports that she might be able to practise; she tells me that she uses her bicycle every day and that she used to ride for very long distances, even hundreds of kilometres. She also practised a Vietnamese combat sport in a club near where she lived. Because of her operation, and from fear of traumatic shocks that might cause an epileptic fit, she gave up combat sports. Chloé is also taking care of herself in dietary terms—we then talk about cooking and meals. She tells me that she has been a vegetarian since she was fourteen; she adopted this diet over twenty years ago. Her mother cooked for her and her two sisters and she has always been greatly concerned with it in her own way; at midday she would eat some pasta and ham, and in the evening, vegetable soup, yoghurt, and fruit. Her mother was not an excellent cook, but she took care of her children and, despite Chloé's criticisms of her, the image that very gradually appears is of a highly ambivalent mother absorbed by her occupation as a maths teacher and the education of her three daughters. For many years, between the ages of five and thirteen, every day at midday her mother would take all three of them to the seaside fairly close to their home and they would eat after having a swim—some pleasant memories are beginning to emerge.

I continue by addressing the relationship between her mother and her father and how they chose each other; she tells me that her father was an engineer; I then suggest an interpretation that makes her laugh a lot: they probably chose each other because they both liked maths. In this way, I encourage her to learn laughter and to distance herself from the parental superego. We then return to technical procedure, because suddenly I think of a technique for overcoming her difficulty in remembering.

Information reaches her more easily by sensory and motor paths and I form the hypothesis that the visual and auditory sensory circuits are partly damaged on several levels, which also involves some disconnections in the psychic domain (c.f., my interview with the neurosurgeon above). Chloé confirms this hypothesis to me and I then think that the only way of remembering would be to use the motor path: she would take some notes on index cards for each book she reads every week and in this way, by writing with her hand, she will be able to remember what she has read. She confirms to me that when she writes, she remembers what she has written. We decide together that she will use the fingers of her hand to remember what she has read (procedural memory); she will write the summaries on index cards that she will arrange in a box. That will help her to reply more easily to the readers who ask her for information about the publication of new books.

At the end of the session, she returns to her adolescence; from the age of seventeen, she wandered all over Europe from squat to squat. We may have the opportunity to return to this particular history of wandering.

The recall technique uses the motricity of the hand and the motor cortices

After the Christmas holidays, Chloé arrives smiling and relaxed for her session. I greet her with a smile, and ask what has happened since the session before the holidays. She tells me that she was experiencing enormous tension and that she had an epileptic fit in the night at home. Thinking aloud, I tell her that the tension created in the last session had generated strong emotions that had increased the neuronal excitation, and that by not being mentally elaborated, the neurones had been discharged in an epileptic fit.

Chloé agrees with this; we must continue to work to reduce her fits as much as possible, but her doctor has informed her that these will not end until two years after her operation. It is obvious that this is only the medical viewpoint. Medicine only assesses the condition, whereas I assess the reasons for the onset of a higher quantum of mental and neuronal excitations.

Throughout the session, we try to construct her history together ("story-telling") in order to assemble gradually the necessary elements for the psychic work. I encourage her to talk about her childhood, the Christmas celebrations, what relations she has had with her two sisters, Catherine and Sylvie, and with her mother and father. She does not like Christmas celebrations because her mother and all the family members on her mother's side have never given her what she wanted as a present. Today she prefers celebrating with her boyfriend André and some other friends, but no one in this circle celebrates Christmas or New Year.

Concerning her work, she tells me that she has followed my advice and written some index cards to remind herself of the content of the books she has read with a view to recommending them to readers at the library. It seems that this writing technique, connecting visual words and written words with the hand (motor cortex), enables her to recall the content of books better. I had thought about using the motor path to supplement the visual word that was not retained in her memory, based on the hypothesis that the hand's motricity could create some new complementary synaptic connections that would be more effective. She confirms to me that she has found this very useful and that she is going to continue with this experiment.

Chloé also talks to me about the loss of linguistic reflexes; when she talks with the library readers, she can only remember the first question they ask and tries to answer it. She knows what all the words mean but cannot use them in conversation.

I nevertheless register that, during our conversations, Chloé replies to me very easily when we are evoking memories or she is talking about herself, her work, and her relationships with others. Recalling the psychic and emotional experience activates the associative neuronal networks.

It is true that our conversation has to use only short sentences that express a single thought. The dual relationship is a substantial aid in mental recovery, which is not possible in the context of the neurologist's usual work.

Associations of ideas begin to return and the epileptic fits diminish

The session marks an important turning-point in Chloé's psychotherapy. As usual, I have taken the initiative of conducting the whole session using questions that address every aspect of her current life, to get her used to evoking current memories increasingly quickly so as to awaken in her working memory some associative capacities, first between events by referring to a world (such as the world of her work), and then by developing the capacities for connections between the various worlds of her present-day life so that she can move more and more quickly from one to the other; in other words, to increase the density of the preconscious (Marty).

I noticed that Chloé had difficulty concentrating on current events in order to evoke them and connect them with other events; she also had some difficulty elaborating on these events, using adjectives to amplify descriptions and making contact with the feelings of the experience of these events.

I concentrate first on the world of her work, about which she has complained a great deal because she has felt misunderstood by her two colleagues there. It seems that, now, after the New Year celebrations, she can work better. Her two colleagues and friends are more able to deal with her epileptic fits if they occur during her working day.

She reminds me that she is having an epileptic fit only once a week or even once a fortnight; this is generally happening at home. In this connection, I ask her some questions to find out whether her body is sending her an alarm signal before the fit and how she interprets this warning sign. She finishes by noting that, just before the fit, her gaze becomes blurred and that the fit follows one hour later, which enables her to lie down in her bed to avoid having an accident. This lucidity about the relationship to her body is a favourable factor for what follows, to the extent that I establish that she is listening to her body, interpreting the signals sent by the brain.

I then move on to other subjects, such as her circle of friends, and then shortly afterwards to her relations with her parents. Concerning her friends, she tells me that she has driven them away insofar as she has only kept the friends who showed themselves to be supportive after her operation, and that the others form part of her circle of relationships but are not her friends. She explains that women are much more sensitive to her condition than men. We make some observations together on the difficulties men have with perceiving a woman's sensitivities.

She has very good relations with her boyfriend André, who lives with her, and this is a pretext for me to mention the presents that she was given at the end of the year. She returns to this subject, which we had already mentioned, to explain to me that in the Christmas and New Year celebrations, she did not have any presents because she does not want any, but André always gives her suitable gifts, such as music CDs that she likes. I then continue by talking about music (this is another pretext for learning semantic associative connections); she tells me again that she likes punk music. She has very recently become capable of listening to music, but that before, music was just an uninterpretable noise. The fact that she can give a meaning to what she hears in the musical domain tells me that there is probably some development of the synaptic connections in the auditory sensory cortex.

Talking about the other presents, I take up the associative chain of the family to return to her father and mother; her father was never able to give her a present, but both her parents come to see her. I ask her to specify whether he is affectionate with her and if he embraces her. She tells me that he is affectionate but always true to form—a stranger. Her mother has given her very few presents, mainly books. Books were so precious to her that she has never dared to underline a sentence in order to take it in. She put covers on them and arranges them carefully. She had so few books that all her reading was done from her school library. I take this opportunity to ask her if she ever received pocket money and, if so, from what age. She tells me she never had any pocket money and it was only from the sixth year of secondary school that she began to receive some once a month in a very limited way.

I ask her about her reading, while taking care not to wound her by asking questions that might emphasise that she does not remember what she reads. I ask her if her recent reading has inspired any thoughts; she replies that it makes her think of the cold. I have noted on several occasions that she attaches great importance to the atmosphere and climate of a book, but never talks to me about characters in this book (which refers us back to the current predominance of the right hemisphere in her functioning). I associate myself to the current cold of the winter period that we are going through and I mention the cold of her parents' town where she lived; I tell her that it must be much colder there than in Paris. She hates the cold, and suddenly, during the last ten minutes of the session, memories of her earlier life stream into her mind.

She lived in the South of France until the age of ten and then moved to a town in north-eastern France, where her mother taught in a secondary school; this was very difficult for her because she was teased about her accent and it took her two years to adjust to it. She had been top of the class but this situation changed when she moved school; it was an elitist school that selected pupils for the competitions of the Grandes Écoles. She found it difficult to adapt and, in the penultimate year she was removed by the teachers, which enabled her to go to a nicer school and to succeed brilliantly in the baccalaureate. The atmosphere of this school enabled her to form bonds with her fellow pupils and to work less stressfully. Evoking all these events in an associative way and on her own initiative (which she felt), and moving back and forth between past and present suggest to me that the beginnings of an associative work, an objective followed since this therapy began, is very modestly being achieved. Of course, I congratulated Chloé for doing this work, and on her newly acquired capacities (narcissistic enhancement).

One year later, psychodynamic conflicts emerge

In this particular session, I initially remember Chloé's silence towards me as if she were disturbed by my questions that were aimed only at helping her to instigate the associative chains to enable her to recover a good mental functioning.

She looks at me and finally tells me that my questions are disturbing her and that she does not want to talk to me. I then realise that we are in a relationship in which some conflict is appearing—possibly a repetition of memories, or repressed or preconscious behaviours. I then ask her with whom she usually behaves in that way and she replies to me very gently that it is her mother and that she does not want to answer the questions. I then explain to her the difference between the maternal relationship and the relationship in therapy—*above all, the process of repetition in the transference.*

She understands better what I am saying to her, and therefore my intention; she then replies by bringing up a painful time in her past that relates to the present situation: her difficulty in trusting the other. She mentions the loss of a close friend called Christine, whom she knew when she was in the fifth year of secondary school, and who committed suicide at the age of twenty-two.

I then adopt an attitude of "intersubjective" intervention by telling her about an episode from my past that was very painful for me that was reactivated in the countertransference relationship. I experienced an identical episode when my friend Paul suddenly died at the age of thirteen from a long illness. Bringing this up reminded me, like Chloé, of the lack of confidence that I have felt throughout my life since my friend's death.

The last part of the session was extraordinary, because Chloé revealed that for two weeks she had been able to hear music, after many months in which music had only been an incomprehensible and painful noise for her. I had already observed this, as mentioned above, but now it is confirmed in a more conscious way. It is obvious that the therapeutic sessions have managed to develop a protective shield of sound that has enabled—according to my hypothesis—a recovery of the cortices associated with the hearing and harmonisation of sounds. Wernicke's area, essential for understanding human language, is situated in the secondary auditory area. The main cerebral regions (for language) are situated in the region immediately adjacent to the auditory cortex.

Continuing with the dynamic relationship and remembering

Chloé goes back to the previous session and confirms what I had sensed, namely some aggression towards me. The memory of her close friend who committed suicide had created a hostile atmosphere, directed at me. In this session, I had facilitated the activation of associative chains relating to this drama, by wishing her a good trip for the following Monday in her parents' town, where she was going with her boyfriend. Chloé had looked at me for a long time while revealing her sense of guilt towards her deceased friend, because it was then that she had met her current boyfriend, which had distanced her from her friend when she had needed her to be there. She felt guilty for having abandoned her.

Our interviews continue, and towards the end of the first quarter of the second year of therapy, Chloé seems much more lively and available in the relationship than previously. She smiles and her faint Germanic accent has almost disappeared. Her speech flows faster and she seems to access words and expressions more quickly. She tells me that she has had a dream:

> *She is in a huge flat that is unfamiliar, and her whole family is together; her sisters Catherine and Sylvie, her mother, and her father with his feet under the table, as usual. There is a kind of increased family closeness in this dream and Chloé, who is happy, is going to give a present; she starts making some dough to bake a cake. Her mother tastes the dough and states that it is not sweet enough; Chloé is unhappy and goes away.*
>
> The dream continues: *her paternal grandmother, whom she loves very much, appears (she died around four years ago); she is very happy to find her grandmother again and never wants to see her mother again, she seems completely categorical on this point.*

The therapy has enabled her to access a maternal imago that she loves, and my role will gradually change in the future sessions; as Chloé herself is in the process of changing. The perception-consciousness system (Freud) is growing; her field of consciousness is increasing.

We continue the session by talking about her many visits to doctors; she wants to stop her antidepressant treatment. I advise her to observe a gradual withdrawal process that will be indicated to her by her doctor; it is two months since she began taking this antidepressant and she thinks it is affecting her libido. She recently rediscovered the pleasure in reading that had disappeared since her operation. She also likes meeting her group of friends, listening to rock music—we laugh a lot because I tell her that I do not know any of this modern music, especially not hard rock (self-irony). We try to make a list of the things that she can enjoy in life without really addressing genital sexuality. I continue by referring to the problem of her boyfriend André, who ended their relationship over a month ago now; this is a separation that may be painful to experience, and I wonder if she is prepared for it.

I ask her the question in order to discover whether this is not going to be too hard for her. To my amazement, she replies to me that everything is fine, that she accepts this separation and she is not jealous. Also, her ex-boyfriend André's girlfriend with whom Chloé shares a flat lives in the same town as her parents and Chloé does all she can to help André to spend at least a few days in the week with this girlfriend. This emotional distance worries me, just as it surprises her friends; Chloé is not jealous, and she never has been of either Catherine or Sylvie. She thinks that she has everything she wants when she wants it because she is not in need of anything. I draw her attention to the lack of emotional manifestation, suggesting that the operation may have affected the emotional centres—she does not think so. Is this alexithymia connected with the deferred action of the operation, or a suppression of emotions connected with the jealousy towards her sisters?

We continue by talking about her reading as a child and adolescent; amid much laughter, we criticise the Countess of Ségur. She preferred to read Jules Verne.

In her occupation as a librarian, she is especially concerned with art books and young people's books. In mid-April she is going to work part-time at the library and one of her colleagues is going to take over the youth section.

I ask about her plans; she replies to me that she prefers to live in the present. Her work has taken up all her time and she no longer has any holiday to take. This is why she lives in the present rather than the future. She prefers to have more time to travel, for example.

We are reaching the end of the session, because we have now been working for an hour; I ask whether the session has tired her; she smiles at me and seems completely relaxed. We part, arranging a meeting in two weeks' time.

During the session, she tells me that she has seen the neurosurgeon and had an MRI scan and that it seems that what remains of the tumour has not increased in size. My colleague asked her if she was continuing her treatment with me, and she confirmed this to him.

Assessment of the treatment after two years

Chloé has changed a great deal and I would like to indicate the progress made.

- First: her flow of speech has considerably increased; she quickly accesses the most ordinary vocabulary.
- Second: her Germanic accent has disappeared, the synaptic connections have restored the French intonation; this point has been confirmed by the psychoneurologist.
- Third: Chloé is comfortable in her body; she moves easily across the space, and sits down smiling in her armchair.

I ask her if she knows that things are going much better; she answers me, smiling, and agrees with all the findings because she states that, thanks to the speech flow that she has recovered, she has been able to rebuild friendly social relations and end her isolation. She no longer takes notes to remind herself of books to recommend to readers. She thinks that it is the work we are doing that has contributed to improving her current state. I tell her that the work we are doing is a joint work and that she has participated well in it.

She relates to me two dreams; in the first: *she is with her epileptologist doctor, whom she knows, but his face is black in colour; he asks her to wait a little because, he says, from his window he will be able to supervise the car park where there are some cars*. Her dream stops there; she does not understand it.

We begin the associations: I suggest to her some associative chains with which she may of course disagree: supervising the car park in a building of this kind could mean that we are in a dangerous suburb; has she ever lived in this kind of suburb? She replies to me that this was ten years ago in her native town. The blackness of her doctor's face may signify the reflection of the sombre preoccupations on her doctor's face concerning her state of health at that time, and she tells me that she thinks that the glioma may have begun to develop at that time; she informs me that the glioma was growing at a rate of 8 per cent per year.

In the second dream, *she is quarrelling with her boyfriend André, and does not understand this very well because they have never quarrelled*.

We discuss this at great length and finally address her relationship with André, which I had not previously dared to mention for fear of prematurely introducing an emotion[5] connected with the sadness of the separation, as he had left her for another young woman. I am surprised that over all these years they never should have quarrelled, as if it were difficult for her to have a conflictual and ambivalent relationship. As for André, he has two women as I tell her—one 400km away from Paris and the other in Paris, which is she herself. I say this to her in jest; she laughs, and protests because she does not live with André, she no longer has a relationship with him. She tells me that André recently stated that he preferred not to get married, not to have money, and to live as in adolescence. She realises that André is very immature; Chloé is withdrawing slightly and beginning to mourn her relationship. She has decided to take a holiday with a female friend.

We mention her current social life and network of friends. She talks animatedly about the life that she is leading: arranging meetings with her friends every other month, leading groups connected with her immediate local area—she seems happy with her life. She does not want to think about the future, preferring to live in the present; my clinical experience has confronted me several times with the psychic changes caused by illness. There are some people who suddenly give a meaning to their life under the impact of a grave threat to their existence. Chloé's glioma has caused this transformation. I have also often noticed that the restoration of the psychosomatic unity due to the medical and psychical repair has led patients to lead their lives differently—their perceptions of themselves and of others changed by their recovery.

In summary, I think about the "mirror effect" of the earliest beginnings of our relationship, with her hesitant approach and difficulties in verbal expression, and I find that now I am no longer tired at the end of our sessions. I invent a new concept for my British colleagues in the Neuropsychoanalysis Society: "to be a good enough mirror". I point out, following Marty's teachings and Ferenczi's clinical practice, that in psychosomatic therapy we play the role of a benevolent and empathetic mother, reactivating the baby's early attachment relations. This is not a classical transference relationship; a maternal attitude of this kind facilitates the narcissistic repair of the psychosomatic unity. The therapist's maternal "mirror" allows connections to be rebuilt between behaviours, emotions, and thoughts and enables the psychic apparatus to be repaired.

Chloé returned for a final session after a month away; she had ended her therapy herself because she could no longer pay for her sessions. I had written to her to suggest that she resume her therapy free of charge and she had told me that she accepted in exchange for books. In fact, we had travelled a long way and it was time to take a break; for how long I did not know—it was for Chloé to resume contact to continue the therapy at her request. The pretext given related to more complex problematics on which we would have to work later; the psychic dynamics were becoming livelier and I was happy about this. Chloé needed a rest.

She seemed more relaxed than a month earlier; she had taken a holiday but she had noticed that the epileptic fits were more frequent (around twice a week). She thought that this was due to the medication; she was to meet the doctor soon to change the prescription.

Chloé knows when the fit is about to happen and at that time she loses consciousness for around twenty minutes (for five minutes, she has some uncoordinated movements then loses consciousness). She is very happy because it seems that the therapeutic work has helped her to pursue her path. After my questions before the treatment was ended a month ago, I had talked to her about jealousy and about my surprise that she had not reacted when her boyfriend André had preferred another young woman as a girlfriend. The work of mental elaboration had been done; Chloé remembers having been jealous of her two sisters when they had bigger helpings of meat than she did.

She has some dreams that she does not remember, but she now feels that she is angry with her boyfriend who has left her. It seems that gradually the aggressive drives are manifesting; she went to her parents' town without meeting them. She stayed with some friends she had known for about twelve years. She also went on a bicycle ride in the Morvan region with another young woman, and she is very happy about this. We address another subject: she talks about her "gaps", which are in understanding what she calls "notions", such as subjectivity or forgetting words to which she does not have access but recognises if she consults a dictionary. I suggest to her activating the auditory memory by reading the texts aloud, since the first constitution of the memory is done on the basis of hearing words and repeating them rather than writing them.

She promises me that she will follow these recommendations and we move on to some discussion exercises that enable her to activate her memory, mastery of words, and capacity to develop arguments. We talk about anarchy, which she explains to me at length, as well as the history of the anarchist movements. She promises to give me a book on this subject and we move on by referring to her commitment to such a path by opposition to her family environment to which she never wants to return; she wants to cut off all ties with her parents.

She started rebelling against her parents while listening to music—it was her way of becoming independent and freeing herself of the family yoke. We can now better understand the psychic dimension of the auditory problems.

She promises to explain to me what this music is and we both laugh about my ignorance in this area. With the gradual reconstitution of the psychosomatic unity, the oedipal problematic has reappeared.

We part, having arranged a meeting in two weeks' time to make a final assessment before our separation. Chloé does not return but sends me a very nice letter to wish me a happy New Year.

* * *

Appendix to the case

At the beginning of her psychosomatic therapy, Chloé brought a book, in which she had underlined many paragraphs because her working memory capacity was very limited, which resulted in her being unable to remember what she had read. One of these passages was concerning a female patient called Barbara, who was described as mentally retarded, but who discovers how to heal all alone:

> She had a visual disability as well. Her span of vision was so narrow that when she looked at a page of writing, she could only take in a few letters at a time. But these were not her most debilitating problems. Because the part of her brain that helps to understand the relationships between symbols was not functioning normally, she had trouble understanding grammar, mathematical concepts, logic, and cause and effect. She could not distinguish between "the father's brother" and "the brother's father". The double negative was impossible for her to decipher. She could not read a clock because she could not understand the relationship between the hands. She literally could not tell her left hand from her right, not only because she lacked a spatial map but because she could not understand the relationship between "left" and "right". Only with extraordinary mental effort and constant repetition could she learn to relate symbols to one another. (Doidge, 2007, p. 29)

In relation to a school that Barbara later started for people suffering from weaknesses in brain function:

> One boy with this problem was always frustrated, because his thoughts came faster than he could turn them into speech … He was a very social person yet could not express himself and so remained silent much of the time … he began to doubt himself. (ibid., p. 38)

Through some exercises developed at Arrowsmith School, Barbara helped some patients who had speech difficulties associated with a deficiency in the Broca region: "Since expending the extra mental effort to support a weak area seems to divert resources from strong areas, a person with a Broca's problem may also find it harder to think while talking" (pp. 40–41).

The following concerns treatment following a cerebrovascular accident.

Based on his work with plasticity, Taub has discovered a number of training principles: training is more effective if the skill closely relates to everyday life; training should be done in increments; and work should be concentrated into a short time, a training technique Taub calls "massed practice", which he has found far more effective than long-term but less frequent training (ibid., pp. 155–156).

Concerning the orbito-frontal lesion of a patient who had recently lost his mother:

> Mr. L. did not get better all at once. He had first to experience cycles of separations, dreams, depressions, and insights—the repetition, or "working through," required for long-term neuroplastic change. New ways of relating had to be learned, wiring new neurons together, and old ways of responding had to be unlearned, weakening neuronal links ... We all have defense mechanisms, really reaction patterns, that hide unbearably painful ideas, feelings, and memories from conscious awareness ... In analysis Mr. L. began to have opportunities to reexperience painful autobiographical memories of searching for his mother that had been frozen in time and dissociated from his conscious memories. Each time he did so he felt more whole as neuronal groups encoding his memories that had been disconnected were connected. (ibid., pp. 232–233)

In giving me this book, Chloé was wanting to help me to understand her condition, and I am still grateful to her for this help.

CHAPTER THREE

Claude: "The Little Prince's heartache"

"And that is how I made the acquaintance of the little prince" (Saint-Exupéry, 1974, p. 13), who arrived at my consulting practice one day in 2003, referred by my colleague in the endocrinology department with the recommendation of giving him some support in the difficult period he was going through. Claude had been her son's teacher and she talked to me with great feeling about this schoolmaster's pedagogical and emotional qualities.

At the hospital, the doctors pay a lot of attention to our patients' somatic symptoms and, as medicine is divided into many disciplines, any problem with an organ or a somatic function is treated by the doctor or doctors in another department. But is that adequate for understanding the illness or illnesses, or, above all, for understanding the patients? Why has the illness developed? Why not link life events with the emergence of somatic problems, as I do in integrative psychosomatics?

My medical colleagues only consider patients' medical histories and also, in some cases, their behaviours, in order better to assess how far the medical recommendations are being followed. In psychosomatics, the fundamental question is: what role is the illness playing in the patient's psychosomatic economy? If the psychosomatician is not associated with the medical observations in a complementary way, only the symptoms are studied, which does not always help the patient; this is what happened to Claude. First though, I must set out in detail his somatic problems, which occurred in the 1980s.

Claude was born in 1942, and the history of his illness began in 1987 (when he was forty-five years old): he was taken to hospital because of a heart attack, in a provincial town where he was spending his holidays. The coronary angiography (an x-ray of the arteries supplying the heart) revealed a stenosis of the anterior interventricular artery (a coronary artery). His medical history revealed a mild tobacco addiction, his mother's coronary artery disease from the age of fifty, and his father's arterial hypertension, complicated by a cerebral vascular accident (stroke). The lipid assessment carried out during Claude's hospitalisation in the endocrinology department showed a total cholesterol of 2g/l, which is a reasonable indicator.

However, his file does not reveal any enquiry into the circumstances that preceded the heart attack; only the current symptoms and his parents' medical histories are considered. This is the usual method of approach in medicine. This information is incomplete, in my view, since it does not take into consideration life events in connection with somatic disorders—what might have happened to this patient?

I continue the medical account: the development of this infarction was initially favourable with no disturbances in the heart rate nor any haemodynamic complication. Taking account of the ventricular dilatation and an ejection fraction of around 40 per cent, anticoagulant treatment was initiated and maintained over the long-term. Claude had returned to work in the new academic year, in September 1987, and then suffered from what seemed to be a vasovagal problem with no development of the coronary illness in December 1987. What had happened? No information.

Claude had consultations in February and June 1988, and some progress was recorded. He was seen again in consultation two years later, and the functional progress appeared to be reasonable without any signs of angina or cardiac deficiency. The ejection fraction was over 55 per cent and the hypercholesterolaemia had abated, falling to 1.80g/l. Claude had been hospitalised again four years later for a ventricular tachycardia accompanied by an anginal pain that did not respond to nitroglycerin (a standard treatment for angina). This rhythmic disturbance had been reduced and controlled by treatment; angiography did not reveal any lesions on the arteries. By contrast, the ejection fraction had dropped to 30 per cent and a higher left ventricular pressure was recorded. It was then decided to implant a cardiac stimulator to help the patient by preventing ventricular tachycardias. The patient was reviewed regularly every six months for heart monitoring; in 1995, a stable condition was recorded both in functional terms and in the clinical and electrocardiographic (ECG) data. At the end of the year, a brain embolism (stroke) occurred with speech disturbance, which resolved in forty-eight hours, and the carotid axes showed non-significant atheromatous lesions (plaques in the arteries of the neck). The brain scan turned out to be normal and the echocardiogram confirmed a left ventricular dilatation. Claude then returned to his teaching work in extremely painful conditions. He was hospitalised in 1997 for an atrial tachycardia; this disturbance in rhythm was connected with a weight loss of some kilos over several weeks, after which a new thyroid assessment was made, which revealed a hyperthyroidism, probably in connection with the treatment that he had been prescribed. The thyroid assessment had revealed in echography a normal-sized thyroid gland without nodular formation or adenopathy. During this hospitalisation, further monitoring of the left ventricular ejection fraction had been carried out, and this was 15 per cent. Following these findings, the patient had been advised to stop work, which was no longer compatible with his cardiovascular situation since his health and safety were at risk.

Meeting Claude

When I met Claude, he was sixty-one years old and, according to his medical file, his cardiac health had been constantly declining since 1987, and I suppose, long before this date. He also suffered from hyperthyroidism, and my clinical experience suggested to me that he had suffered from constant stress over very long periods. In fact, the thyroid gland, in conjunction with the psychic apparatus, is the organ that absorbs daily and constant stress; if this organ malfunctions, we can put forward the hypothesis of extreme psychic fragility because the mental apparatus has not been able to absorb the quantum of daily excitation, and I needed to find out the reasons why. I formed the hypothesis of a deficiency in the psychic apparatus, since the thyroid gland, as well as other vital functions, had been strongly attacked; once again, the body was taking over.

Claude is a short man, who is waiting for me in our waiting room with the other patients in the department, and I go up to him to invite him to come with me into my office. He sets me wondering—I do not really know whom I am facing; it is difficult at first to establish any contact with him. He appears both close and distant. Who is he? He has come to see me because he has faith in my colleague and thinks I might be able to help him. Alongside me in my office I had one of my training students who seemed to be interested in Claude. This student has attended all my interviews with this patient, over the past two years. I will often be making reference to Saint-Exupéry because, as we will see, my patient was very fond of this author.

Claude states that he is well now and announces that he is gradually attaining a degree of inner calm. He is professionally at a standstill and regrets it deeply because he is very attached to his pupils; he now lives alone in his flat with his dog. In many sessions over the following year we talked about nothing but his dog, which was another way of talking about him. He is no longer completely alone thanks to this animal, which acts as a protective shield. Of course, the curious question of the psychoanalyst who converses with his patient about his pet can be posed, but it will very quickly be understood that the unconscious is revealed more easily in this way; the pet often fulfils the role of a protective shield and external object.

Claude expresses his recurrent difficulty in making choices, for example in improving his bathroom, and making decisions as if he were waiting for some authorisation or permission. He is convinced of the absurdity of these blocks, as a form of powerlessness to act. The conflict between the ego and the superego gradually appears; his superego is strongly characterised by the conflictual relationship with his father, who was the person he always had to ask for everything and who never replied yes, but often "we will see." I sense that Claude is deeply helpless and very vulnerable, with a sort of powerlessness to act and react and to take charge of himself. This behaviour also makes us refer to his capacity to explore the environment and to experience his illness passively; it is obvious that a masochistic dimension is at work but this requires further exploration, as does the superego.

As Claude talks about his father, it becomes clear that he is very attracted by him, revealing his problematic on the negative side of the Oedipus complex; we discover that in a sort of hysterical identification with his mother he shares some of her somatic symptoms. Passive tendencies prevail; it is easier to understand his masochistic dimension and his capacity to deal with all the somatic problems. The pathological masochistic dimension is not always to be assessed negatively in our patients; in this case, it is life masochism rather than death masochism, as so well described by Rosenberg (1991).

I wonder about the kind of relationship he may have had with his pupils as a teacher—that will recur later in our interviews. For the moment, I begin to understand that all the psychic functioning is dominated by this unconscious quest for passivity. He lost his father several years ago, but the mourning does not seem to have been carried out and the unconscious conflict seems to be continuing, because he states very forcefully that he had never confronted his father and that he prefers to adopt the current attitude. He refuses, he says, ever to be buried in the family mausoleum, and would prefer to be cremated. He feels uneasy when he goes near his parents' former house. I remember from our conversation the pathological mourning that continues to influence his current functioning while probably aggravating the symptoms, since this process expends energy.

Initiating the mourning process on the therapeutic level seems to me to be an appropriate beginning for gradually easing the intrapsychic tensions caused by the paternal conflict; by doing so, a better fusion of the drives and an expression of aggressive impulses outside the ego might ultimately be obtained. A relaxation of the superego would facilitate the task.

Claude's account

Claude begins by telling us that he has seen his cardiologist the day before, then talks about his total cholesterol tests that continue to fall and have reached 1.3g, which is too low. The test laboratory has pointed this out to him but the cardiologist said only that it might be necessary to review the "Tahor 40", an anti-cholesterolaemia medicine (statin); he is taking eight medicines daily. Better regulation seems necessary. Somatic patients sometimes use all their sessions to talk about their problems and medicines as if the psychic work could not be done; that sometimes takes several months or years and a psychosomatician must be patient.

Claude complains of difficulties in sleeping, specifically with falling asleep. The degree of excitation that cannot be elaborated hinders the regression necessary for sleep. In the best case, the therapeutic relationship might be able to help to reduce the internal tensions, but Claude is very rarely available and we only meet at long intervals.

At the very beginning of our meeting Claude was having difficulty associating, then gradually associations appeared relating to his fear of death. He mentions first the episode of his heart attack in the Doubs region (at the end of March), and his stay in the resuscitation unit of which he has a painful memory; then, a tachycardia attack when he entered "F" street in Paris, which he uses regularly but now avoids. For the time being, he cannot remember what happened to him in this street in his past; he shares with me his fear of not waking up when he goes to sleep, and then his fear when he goes past Cochin hospital.

His body has a memory of all his traumas and they return periodically; I have often noted that when the psychosomatic unity is deeply disturbed, the central nervous system sends the patient's ego many messages that could be interpreted as somatic anxiety—an alarm signal. The evening and night are therefore difficult, because the somatic unconscious, the bio-regulation markers, and memories of past episodes, remind him of all the threatening incidents accompanied by fear of death. The ego capacities are still too fragile to deal with the emotional onslaught connected with the heart problems; this is understandable, it is not for the time being repression that is operating. The work of elaboration can only be done because the patient has difficulties in linking the psychic representations and the emotions. We are confronted with emotions of which the circuits are activated by the somatic unconscious. The anxiety is translated by avoidance behaviours, and cardiac accelerations that the doctors perceive very well.

Nevertheless, there is some improvement; from a cardiac perspective, the extrasystoles (ectopic, or "extra" heartbeats) are only at 3 per cent now, indicating a recovery that may have been facilitated by the psychotherapeutic support. Claude's cathexes in social or other activities and his satisfactions in life are still very limited, but the new awareness is progressing, even if he has some difficulty allowing himself to go to the cinema; he feels a bit alone to go out in this way.

A new year begins; we continue

The therapeutic process evolves gradually, and we move from a factual account to a more mentalised discourse; the patient's memory is returning. Claude talks to me again about his insomnia and the tensions he is currently experiencing, and he reports a dream:

> *He goes to his parents' house and, in the entrance to the garden, he sees some paper roses in the place of the hydrangea bed.*

He does not associate immediately; he talks to me first about his heart problems in the last three months and the analysis of the diagrams from his defibrillator; in two months he has had more than sixteen incidents corrected by this device. He is taking "cordarone" to regulate the cardiac arrhythmia and is worried about the consequences on his thyroid functioning. He is also worried about the long-term need to replace his defibrillator, because the batteries will expire; at present, there is no means of recharging the batteries by infrared. It will therefore be necessary to change his defibrillator that is worth over €200,000. It seems that the French annual funds cannot provide for more than the 2,500 devices that are currently implanted every year.

> Grown-ups [doctors] love figures. When you tell them that you have made a new friend, they never ask you any questions about essential matters. They never say to you, "What does his voice sound like? What games does he love best? ..." Instead, they demand: "How old is he? How many brothers has he? How much does he weigh?" (Saint-Exupéry, 1974, pp. 17–18)

The Little Prince thus mischievously criticises the adults who are interested not in the person but in the numbers; the quantitative takes precedence.

My approach with Claude is very often educative, as if to prepare him mentally. I put forward the hypothesis that somatic anxieties connected with his trauma are resurfacing at night and causing him cardiac arrhythmias because of the emotion being released. The emotional quantum disturbs his cardiac rhythm and I suggest analysing, by association of ideas, the thoughts that are giving rise to the problems in order to mentalise the somatic excitations—to put things into words. He associates very easily about the red of the roses in his dream, which initially reminds him of a traumatic event in which a young child at his school had an accident that he witnessed and that he cannot forget—there at last is one of the traumas that appears. In his associations, he mentions the years 1979 and 1980, during which he had taken up *The Little Prince* as a book for these primary school pupils. He had asked his pupils to do some drawings to illustrate the reading of the book that had been chosen both by the pupils and himself, then recorded some cassettes that he has kept and has not yet had the courage to listen to. He tells me that the psychiatrist he had consulted some years ago had advised him to destroy these cassettes to forget the past, but he wonders how the past can be forgotten, especially a past that is so strongly cathected. I reply that it is impossible to forget the past by destroying an educational aid to which he had devoted a lot of time and emotion, and that the main problem is in fact gradually mourning a painful past that involved important emotions. He begins to understand that the psychic mechanism of mourning is fundamental to being able to perceive what has really happened and to abreact the emotion.

The return to the house mentioned in his dream—his parents' house—reminds him of his relationship with his father; he finds his father distant and he now understands that he wondered whether his father loved him. His father belonged to a very strict generation, brought up harshly himself, who never showed his feelings apart from on one occasion, which was when Claude's mother went into hospital. He remembers having seen his father crying, which greatly surprised him. I tell him that although his father has died, the father he has inside him still exists and that, by analysing the emotional relations he had with him, he can gradually move closer to him and then mourn him. I add that the recollection of his past will gradually enable him to weave connections between the events that have disturbed his equilibrium, and that doing this will aid the mourning process and his overcoming the trauma or traumas that have given rise to all his heart problems; this is my hypothesis and this is the therapeutic objective we followed, what Lacan calls the "direction of the treatment".

Our relations develop and gradually a form of transference relationship seems to be established; Claude brought a book of "psychosomatic medicine" to lend me during the holidays, which is a way of thanking me for the work done and showing his interest in it. He moves closer to me and our work that began over a year ago is fostering a warmer and more empathic relationship.

He remembers the visit by a national educational inspector who came to encourage him following his innovative educational work with *The Little Prince*; he mentions with much feeling and warmth the children in the class to whom he had given sheets of paper to write the story they would invent about the colour red. This colour red is associated with the rose in *The Little Prince*:

> But it happened that after walking for a long time through sand, and rocks, and snow, the little prince at last came upon a road. And all roads lead to the abodes of men. "Good morning," he said. He was standing before a garden, all a-bloom with roses. "Good morning", said the roses. The little prince gazed at them. They all looked like his flower. "Who are you?" he demanded, thunderstruck. "We are roses", said the roses. And he was overcome with sadness. (Saint-Exupéry, 1974, p. 62)

Claude remembers that one of his pupils drew a village that she had called "Montrouge".

He had told the children in his class that he was portraying the snake in *The Little Prince*: "When the little prince arrived on the Earth, he was very much surprised not to see any people. He was beginning to be afraid he had come to the wrong planet, when a coil of gold the colour of the moonlight, flashed across the sand. "Good evening," said the little prince courteously. "Good evening," said the snake" (Saint-Exupéry, 1974, p. 57). The interventions of a psychoanalyst psychosomatician often seem strange; it is, as I point out, a relationship of unconscious to unconscious. I told him that, to me, the snake evoked the snake that tempted Eve in the Bible, I thus referred more to the associative chain of temptation (temptation of his pupils), but it was not the same for him at that time, and I later discovered why this was.

Claude mentions a scene in the novella in which the snake is carrying the little prince in his arms through the desert and finally finds a well. But desire (which?) did not appear in this session; patience is necessary. Where is this snake going to lead us?

I remind him that he had talked to me about his father, who had done his military service in Morocco and who he had told me wore a red kepi. Morocco and the desert are places where his father developed; I thus establish some links between reading his favourite book and his father, since Saint-Exupéry's novella is set in the desert.

We part after Claude has mentioned his visits to my colleague's son, by whom he is invited regularly—he was his pupil, and Claude unfolds before me the list of his relations with many pupils, some of whom are now over forty years old. We wish each other a happy holiday before seeing each other again in January 2005.

The traumas gradually emerge

We have some longer conversations in the New Year, and associative thinking becomes increasingly apparent. The therapy continues on the somatic and the psychic level, but we do not yet have a session completely taken up by psychic functioning.

The summer is approaching and Claude begins by telling me that he feels less oppressed by the heatwave than in the last few days. The weather had been making it difficult for him to go out. He was afraid of having an attack of tachycardia in the street, as had happened before. He addresses the anxiety associated with his attacks and with the idea that this could happen again; he is preoccupied with death.

He remembers that a tachycardia attack had once occurred following a visit from a friend's mother for a week in Paris. This very active woman had exhausted him by her energy and the attack happened shortly after she had left. Claude explains that he was pleased that she had gone. I form the hypothesis of a strong excitation connected with this departure, accompanied by a strong emotional charge; Claude relived a special relationship with his mother, but we were not able to talk about it and the somatic emotion unconnected with mental representations was discharged.

He refuses to mention his personal history, or even to see any connection with his own mother. However, he mentions an important emotion when the man who had saved him thirteen years earlier, and whom he had never seen since, came up to him on a café terrace near his home; Claude had been unwell in the street and this man had helped him greatly at that time. This reunion with his rescuer and their rediscovered bond had evidently disturbed him very much—but why? We are certainly approaching some repressed events in his personal history, but also close relations with a man.

Claude now mentions his relations with children who are in great difficulty that for some of them has led to death.

The history is slowly revealed

Claude states that he is drawn to people who are going through difficult times; he does not know how to say no and protect himself. He therefore forms bonds with young boys who are ill or have had serious accidents. He seems to suffer a lot from these relationships, because he is in direct contact with the child's and the family's suffering. He wants to help them just like the little prince who takes care of his rose on its planet of origin:

> ... in herself alone she is more important than all the hundreds of you other roses ... because it is she that I have watered; because it is she that I have put under the glass globe; because it is she that I have sheltered behind the screen ... because it is she that I have listened to, when she grumbled, or boasted, or even sometimes when she said nothing. Because she is *my* rose. (Saint-Exupéry, 1974, p. 70)

But his intentions are not always well understood, either by his pupils' families or by his colleagues—his behaviour is not understood, and he is assumed to have "paedophilic" intentions. He has undergone criticisms and been distanced in ways that have caused him great suffering.

Claude has experienced severe attacks and accusations over more than fifteen years, and it is now understandable that he has not been able to deal with them; he was a defenceless, helpless man and it is his heart that has suffered from this immensely. The "seductive snake" appears here, revealing unjustified accusations and sufferings.

It is difficult to know how to resist psychically and somatically when the defence system is reduced to behaviour and certain character traits. Claude strangely resembles Marty's patient, Gisèle W. (Marty et al., 1994, pp. 47–74), who also could live only with children; she had remained a child. It is the same for Claude—in this case it is what Marty calls a behavioural neurosis.[1]

Nothing could allay his anxieties, and the whole clinical picture is only a long series of progressive disorganisations of the cardiac function and the thyroid gland. I met Claude much too late, when his cardiac function had reached such a point of decline that I was only able to support him for two and a half years before he broke off our therapeutic conversations, only to be hospitalised again with the indication of a heart transplant; we should remember that the ejection fraction was 15 per cent.[2]

I did not see Claude again, and I deeply regret that my colleagues did not consult me about the transplant indication, because I think that he was not psychically ready to deal with such an ordeal when his heart could no longer pursue its path; he was very much "on his last legs".

When he meets the fox, the little prince asks himself many questions about how to escape his solitude and sadness: "'You do not live here', said the fox. 'What is it that you are looking for?' 'I am looking for men,' said the little prince" (Saint-Exupéry, 1974, p. 65). Just as he leaves the fox, the little prince says to him: "'Goodbye', he said. 'Goodbye', said the fox. 'And now here is my secret, a very simple secret: It is only with the heart that one can see rightly; what is essential is invisible to the eye'" (ibid., p. 70).

Claude never stopped being a little boy who loved other little boys, and he left us. Every time I lose a patient, I am deeply affected.

Strangely enough, I will quote Saint-Exupéry again, because at the time of writing this case history I note that six years have already passed: "And now six years have already gone by" (ibid., p. 89).

CHAPTER FOUR

A hypochondriac patient—the enigma of Damien's somatic problems

For doctors in France today, a hypochondriac problem is an imaginary problem, and therefore non-existent. Is what happens "in the mind" really imaginary? And if it is imaginary, does that mean that this is not a psychic reality that can change thoughts, behaviours, and emotions?

What I will now be considering is how to address these problems in a medical and scientific way. For a psychosomatician psychoanalyst, there is a psychic reality and, as I have shown in the previous cases, we are dealing with some extremely complex problems.

I will now present to you the case of a patient I will call Damien, who consulted doctors for over six years for problems that were described as "hypochondriac".

Damien's problems

Damien read my book *When the Body Displaces the Mind* (Stora, 2007) shortly after it was originally published in French and wanted to meet me to assess his situation. He arranged an appointment with me at La Pitié-Salpêtrière and I talked to Damien and treated him for over four years in my consulting room.

Damien is a fifty-two-year-old man of average height who works as a business consultant; he seems extremely dynamic. I sense that he has an impressive vital tonus. He has what he calls "psychosomatic" problems, and this is why he has come to consult me. As with every somatic patient, I begin by addressing all the symptoms from which he is suffering. I insist on hearing his complaint and his account. He begins by telling about some somatic incidents that have invariably resulted in his being hospitalised. At first there were vestibular problems, vertigo and loss of balance, but no neurological problem was detected. He first went into hospital a long time ago and he no longer remembers the date. The second hospitalisation dates from eight years ago, following a relative's death, but he does not explain the family connection to me. I prefer to let him talk without interrupting his speech because it is not possible to move from a factual account of somatic symptoms to a psychic functioning, which would break the thread of his account. I make a quick assessment of the symptoms: symptoms of metabolic problems (considering biological and echo-Doppler carotid tests), neurological disturbances, and finally gastro-intestinal problems. I prefer to begin by referring Damien to all my colleagues in our hospital's medical departments. It is important to understand the nature of the symptoms and to eliminate or confirm, as necessary, the medical hypotheses one by one.

At the time of writing, I still remember as if it were yesterday that my colleague in the gastroenterology department very quickly called me to tell me his diagnosis: colorectal cancer. This is a patient who consulted doctors for over six years and whose somatic illness was stated to be hypochondriac. This is often due to the patient's attitude misleading the doctor, who very quickly thinks of an "imaginary psychological dimension" without wondering about the symptom itself. Some doctors order tests and when these are negative they feel this confirms their first impression, and pursue no further investigations. In fact, the compartmentalisation of medicine into specialisms is not conducive to a general approach to the patient (see the appendix to this case, below).

I understand their attitude very well and I know that hypochondria can also reveal a somatic illness or a psychic problem, or both, in the long term. The somatic excitations perceived by the central nervous system cause a signal anxiety that leads the patient to consult a doctor, because he thinks he is suffering from an illness that only a doctor can recognise, which for some patients leads to a major medical nomadism with severe disappointments; the patient is seeking the impossible—he wants to put a name to his problems, to reassure himself.

According to the clinical hypothesis I have developed over many years in the endocrinology department, I ask the patient some questions to find out what has happened in the last seven to ten years, which is the time it takes for a tumour to grow following a trauma or events that are difficult to endure. Of course it is also possible, according to psychosomatic hypotheses, to wonder about the probability of a progressive disorganisation, an essential depression and/or a psychic fragility following some traumas. These are questions that a psychosomatician always bears in mind when he is with patients suffering from severe illnesses; it is obvious that these different hypotheses are to be challenged or confirmed in the course of the developing psychotherapeutic conversations and complementary medical investigations.

I continue my interview by appealing to his memories of events over the last ten or fifteen years. Damien remembers that, in the past ten years, he has complained about tiredness but not attached any importance to this problem. In the week after our interview, having been informed of the cancer diagnosis, he was at home where he had already slept more than ten hours and when he woke up he went back to sleep for another hour-and-a-half. He wonders with me what such a symptom can mean, and I put forward the idea that following the announcement of his cancer he had an emotional reaction, causing him to retreat into himself to protect himself from the emotional shock. The tiredness felt over the last few years is probably to be attributed to an excessive consumption of vital energy diverted by the growth of the tumour. It is understandable that the surgeon wants to operate very quickly; shortly after his operation, I visit him in his hospital room to re-establish contact and support him in his ordeal. I then meet the surgeon to receive an account of the course of the operation. I think it is important to visit our patients at their bedside so that they know we are not abandoning them, we are at their side to experience their illness, and, above all, that we are there to help them to carry on with their life.

He did not want to inform any family members except for one of his brothers, his brother-in-law, and his wife. He does not want to tell his daughter, because she is looking for work, or his son, because he will soon have to take an exam; he does not want to upset them. He goes back to his metabolic symptoms; he will soon take an echo-Doppler and have some biological tests, then he will go to the neurology department to understand the reason for his vertigo. Damien thus continues the medical visits that I have recommended to him.

The course of a therapy with somatic patients always follows the same sequence: until the psychosomatic unity is repaired, the patient focuses all the sessions on his symptoms and the repair of his body—with the doctors' help we must *restore the narcissistic completeness of the psychosomatic unity*. This can take several months or years, and the psychosomatician psychotherapist must be patient. Once the repair of the body has been carried out, the therapeutic interviews can be continued in the psychic domain in the place where the regression of the maturation process has stopped, at the point of fixation-regression.

In the neurological examination, my colleague agreed with my hypothesis of vertigo caused by a problem in the circulation of blood towards the brain; there is therefore probably a danger of cerebrovascular accidents, which his wife also suspects because she told him about this some time ago. Damien is worried and tells me that since the last session, in which he had tilted his head backwards and sideways to show me that he was no longer suffering from vertigo, there have been some minor vertigo spells. He is afraid that, as usual, he will repress everything and that the anxiety will manifest itself somatically. Damien has some psychoanalytic knowledge and reading that he later uses as a defence system rather than as an aid to understanding his symptoms. He keeps returning to his fear of vertigo spells that might thwart his new project. His project provides an important elucidation of his symptomatology and his psychosomatic fixations. He wishes, he says, to interest museums and financial sponsors in a plan for some archaeological excavations in sites not currently being mined; this is an exciting project.

I am afraid that the vertigo might manifest itself in the middle of the jungle or the desert; in my opinion he could recruit some colleagues to send in his place and only spend short periods there himself. He has also consulted an ear, nose, and throat specialist who told him that, with a simple manipulation, it would be possible to improve or suppress the vertigo symptoms, caused by otoliths in the inner ear. He is surprised at the anxiety generated by these vertigo spells, whereas he shows great serenity in his struggle against the cancer. The vertigo affects his head and most of his body; he describes himself as someone who tries "to anticipate and control everything." He feels that this anxiety is deep and destabilising for his personality. He is afraid that he has lost his capacity to find quick solutions and the spontaneity of his thinking, because he has always planned everything. His plans might take him away from France for several years, and he wonders how he would be able to undertake a therapy, and at what cost for what benefit? He feels that he cannot control all the risks inherent in such a project.

As he mentions risk, I decide to refer to the risk connected with the cancer and to his remission in the coming years; it will be necessary to wait for several years before a remission can be ascertained. As he has a stoma following his operation, he must observe strict conditions of hygiene. What I say, from my concern to protect his health, frustrates him immensely and he promises me that he will see his oncologist to obtain a medical opinion, in addition to his surgeon's opinion. My warning has suddenly encountered the patient's narcissistic defence, as well as the defence of the drive for mastery (*Bemächtigungstrieb*), because he is thwarted in carrying out his plans. Through its omnipotent quality, the narcissism fuels and reinforces the anal drive; in everything he says, Damien manifests a strong striving for mastery and control that presupposes powerful anal fixations. He talks about his very strict father, who was highly critical, especially towards his wife. He also mentions that, when he was eight years old, his mother threatened to seek a divorce.

In the transference relationship, after my intervention, I assumed the place of the father, to whom he immediately referred since he describes him as a very severe character. I thwarted him with my warnings and he regards me as someone who is preventing him from finishing what he is trying to achieve—just like his father. A severe superego appears here, as well as a fear of emotional abandonment that he experienced as a child.

Damien went to see an oncologist, who completely reassured him about the medical risk of undertaking an extended journey in tropical or desert regions. However, while the doctor did not rule out the possibility that psychic difficulties might play a role, he could not explain the importance of the psychic factor in the somatic risk. Damien therefore decided to withdraw from the riskiest parts of his project; namely, long journeys in regions that pose health risks. Damien still speaks in a very detailed and highly structured way, revealing his obsessional character traits.

He addresses what he considers as the major symptom: his anxiety attacks. Ten days after our previous session, he woke up in the middle of the night with stomach ache, diarrhoea, and a full stoma pocket.

He sleeps alone, because his wife has moved to the country for medical reasons; as he says no more about this for the moment, I prefer to keep quiet and wait, because I sense that this is a very delicate problem. The anxiety wells up, accompanied by tetany all along his legs, then it overwhelms him completely. He is overcome by anxiety and he just has time to swallow a Xanax, which calms him down after fifteen minutes. He makes the connection with the two vertigo attacks, when he was also seized by acute anxiety, diarrhoea, and a need to vomit; all these events occurred at night or very early in the morning. It is therefore evident that the psychic apparatus is being overwhelmed by somatic excitations and the unelaborated endogenous excitations, since he does not report any dream that would have allowed the excitations to be either alleviated or, in the best case, eliminated—he has somatic manifestations of distress.

We meet again, in the new term in September of the same year, and a new trainee student attends our interviews. I draw her attention, just as I have done gradually above, to Damien's narcissistic strivings and the particular cathexis of the active side of the anal drives; I wonder about his defence against passivity when confronted with an authority by which he feels threatened. The underlying hypothesis suggests a strategy of gradually, as soon as it proves possible, exploring the patient's negative Oedipus complex.

The symptoms continue, and as soon as the quantum of daily excitations rises, he experiences vertigo and sometimes has to lie on the floor for more than twenty-four hours at a time; this stops him from thinking.

His recent MRI scan revealed nothing about the vertigo or any neurological problems (we can refer here to hypochondriac symptoms); he adds that he has arranged to see the cardiologist the following week. The psychosomatic psychotherapy continues, but it has not yet brought an end to the anxiety that leads the patient to continue consulting doctors. This medical nomadism is fuelled by the rapid displacement of excitations, for no reason; this is a mute, unmentalised worry.

Damien then relates the most recent events in his life. His wife, who has left to take care of her mother, telephones him to complain about the difficulties of taking care of an old person who is in decline; she adds that she cannot possibly arrive late at school (she is a school-teacher in a small class). Damien reassures her, and does not feel too stressed by this call. The next day, his wife calls him again to ask him to come urgently, because she is going back to hospital because of a glaucoma. Damien then seeks every possible solution to avoid having to join her and to be able to attend his work meetings; he asks some neighbours to take care of his wife's mother and his brother-in-law to look after both his mother and his sister. It is not immediately understandable why he does not go to his wife's bedside, given that he realises the gravity of this incident. Why does he keep a distance? What is he protecting himself from?

He states that, for now, he is managing the situation, and then in the evening things change radically. His twenty-seven-year-old daughter, who is currently sharing his flat while waiting to move somewhere else, comes to join him and they discuss the situation together; he describes her as a strong young woman who, like him, has her feet on the ground. They discuss things together, and during the conversation his daughter's eyes water a little. He is visibly troubled by the emotion shown by his daughter and does not respond; he continues as if nothing had happened and jokes with her in their usual way. Shortly afterwards, he feels some flashes of heat that force him to go and lie down in order to wipe the sweat from his forehead and have his daughter bring him something to eat; he thought he was having a hypoglycaemia attack.

Damien had been hot; the emotional suppression connected with the lack of empathy for the crisis that his wife was undergoing had found a somatic outlet: his body had experienced the impact of his emotion. However, it cannot be said that Damien is alexithymic; he suppresses his emotions and he closes the door to the emotional manifestations of his unconscious.

His psychiatrist had recently changed his medication, and he is now taking Prozac. I draw his attention to the disinhibiting effect of Prozac, but he does not seem to understand, and he also explains that it is not a problem for him, nor for his wife, as sex is not that important. During the session, on several occasions, he makes some verbal slips and confuses "mother" and "wife". At the end of the session, I draw his attention to the fact that every time a problem arises in his life, he turns to his body to find an answer, whereas perhaps we should understand together the psychic repercussions of these events. He seems almost convinced, but wonders what these repercussions may be; I encourage him to continue our conversations because he trusts me. The voluntary nature of the hospital consultations can have either detrimental or beneficial effects for patients.

Psychic recovery during psychotherapy

Following the last session, Damien tells me that he is leaving for the provinces to join his wife. For the first time since our interviews began he talks about his hypertension, and I emphasise that this somatic symptom is accompanied by strong endogenous psychic tensions.

Having returned to Paris, he states very factually, as if a doubt were hovering, that he has chosen his wife, and that despite some ups and down in their relations, he has stayed with her. He does not want to elaborate any further on the state of his marriage; overwhelmed by internal tensions, he turns to another subject.

He prefers to talk about a book that he has recently read; the story brings back some childhood nightmares in which "a beast surprised him and attacked him from behind"; he sees himself as a child in his bed, placed against one of his bedroom walls. The anxiety reappears in the session and he associates it with his childhood night terrors. In his parents' old house, he slept in a first-floor bedroom with two entrances, one being a door into the main part of the building, and the other a staircase that led down into the common areas, in particular a kitchen and junk room—a place of adventure and games that was frightening after dark. He said he had been scared by the thought that a man might be able to enter the bedroom and kill him. He would then stop breathing in order not to be noticed.

He continues his account, describing the scene of a film he saw as a child in which the hero falls into an underground passage under a maharajah's palace. He finds himself in a cave with some imprisoned lepers who approach him. There is a staircase that leads to a closed door, and the hero is rescued when someone opens the door to him just as the lepers are about to reach him.

The thoughts that come spontaneously after these two accounts remind him of the time when his father punished him after he had moved to his secondary school; the dramatic transition from the last year of primary school to the first year of secondary school. Until then he had been a very good pupil and had spent the entire first year of secondary school exploring the whole town in which he lived by bicycle. His academic year had been terrible and he had to repeat it. He had thereby disappointed his father, who had very great ambitions for him and considered him his successor. He was sent to a boarding school a long way from the family home; he could only return home twice a year. He became a very brilliant pupil again, but still bears a very deep trace of this trauma that established him in a passive position towards his father, being under pressure and forced to live far away from him. But psychically, this passive position (negative Oedipus complex) has never been superseded and it is a source of anxiety. In this secondary school, there was a rumour that one supervisor was a paedophile, and abused his power over the children in the dormitory. On the few occasions when he was almost alone in the dormitory at night when all the children had gone home for the weekend, and this man was supervising, he was terrified and could not get to sleep until the supervisor had switched off the light in his bedroom. When he was doing his inspection round, he would hide under the bedclothes and pretend to be asleep.

Brief commentary

His reading, his accounts, his dream, and all his mental representations confirm the existence of a fear of fantasies of homosexual penetration; the hidden staircase in his bedroom that leads down to the kitchen and junk room, the pursuit in the palace basement, and so on confirm the presence of the anal fixation and his fears. This zone has been strongly cathected by the patient, and has been attacked by the cancer. We can refer here to Marty's theory of points of vulnerability–defence and Freud's concept of somatic compliance and, in the context of the psychosomatic meta-model I am presenting, to deficiencies in the articulation of the first and second somatopsychic organisation (Stora, 2011, pp. 120–123). This concerns the interaction between the sympathetic and parasympathetic divisions of the first somatopsychic organisation and the voluntary motor system of the second organisation. This involves five main structures: the locus coeruleus, the hypothalamus, the septal nuclei, and several cortical regions (paracentral lobule, cingulate gyrus, and frontal lobes).

The drive for mastery and the sphincter training will facilitate the integration of complex neuronal sequences interconnecting pleasure and unpleasure, the passive side and active side of the drives, and the progressive differentiation of the psychic apparatus. The constant overwhelming by excitations transmits these to the two somatopsychic organisations that ultimately malfunction, causing many somatic problems in their interconnection with the immune system. This is the hypothesis that I am suggesting to explain the development of colorectal cancer in my patient.

Damien expresses his deep wish to reduce the intensity of his anxieties and is not satisfied with using Xanax to combat this symptom, but he does not want to get involved in a long-term psychotherapy; he is very reticent in this respect. Psychotherapeutic work seems to disturb and worry him. He agrees, however, to continue some interviews at the frequency of one fortnightly session. As for his anxieties, he wonders if these originate from current or past causes; we are gradually making some progress.

Damien embarks on a major reflection, initially obscure, which has emerged from reading a book with a title and an author that he does not mention. For him, the author of the book puts forward two solutions to answer a problem: either find the solution, or remove yourself from the situation and take a step back. Damien then emphasises that he has always been in the position of finding solutions for his close friends and family and even in his occupation. He says that he has always fought, and emphasises that the idea of retiring one day frightens him.

Damien returns to his current symptom, a headache; this symptom appears after he has talked about the future (retirement), *as if to prevent thoughts from arising*. We leave it there; he tells me that he will not be available the following week.

The conflict with women emerges and the associative path continues

Damien arrives at the next session with an anxiety in his stomach that he does not talk about immediately. He thinks that "the last ten days have been a rather positive experience"; things are going better with his mother, stepmother, and daughter. The conflictual dimension with women is beginning to emerge.

He returns to the geographical and emotional separation from his spouse, saying that "the separation was difficult"; I then ask him if he has previously experienced any difficult histories of separation. Damien then relates two major events in his childhood; first, as a child, he heard his mother talking about divorce and remembers how that unsettled him.

He then talks about having been sent away to boarding school at the end of the first year of secondary school, which he felt was totally unfair. He describes his father's cold reaction on seeing his results that year, and his unexplained decision to send him away to school. Damien talks about his lonely times in the dormitory at the weekend when he remained alone—he only returned home twice a year (repetition of the previous sessions).

At the end of the session, Damien talks about a close friend, who shares his enthusiasm for their archaeological research project, while mentioning his impatience, and even his doubts concerning its feasibility. He finally concludes that this is what has been stressing him all morning and spoiling his enjoyment of the good news.

He says at the beginning of the session: "it drains your vital energy; it's incredible." He arrives, giving his blood pressure results, which were very high. He is also going to have a kidney examination, at his doctor's recommendation. I invite him also to have a thorough examination of the coronary arteries.

He has just read the autobiography of a well-known journalist who describes the depression he suffered at the height of his career. It caught him when he was about to take charge of a major radio station (change of job, taking responsibility, depression). Damien draws a parallel with this journalist, because he is also going through a period of change. He says he does not regret his occupation (as a trainer in consultancy), and he thinks he chose it so as to mix with people from his "father's world" who are on the same intellectual level (Grande École and elite).

He returns to an event in his adolescence, linking together his father, his project, and success in life: he tells me how he won a scholarship that enabled him to travel to the countries of northern Europe. He was fifteen years old and had hitchhiked all the way; his father had encouraged him to make this journey. He was very proud of this but talked little about it, and stated one day that he would never have let one of his children travel at that age. I asked him if he had felt in danger on this journey, supposing that something serious might have happened to him. He remembers that he had very little money for the return and that he came back by hitchhiking again, but eating little or next to nothing for a few days, which also reveals an immense capacity for "resilience".

Recounting his journey in the Nordic countries takes him back to his plans for a long journey in tropical countries; for over ten years he has been gathering information and states that he now has enough to travel to this region.

Damien is curious, and at the end of the session he wonders about the differences between intellectual functioning and psychic functioning; the transference is becoming stronger.

In the following month's session, he talks first about his project and the paradox involved in going to carry out excavations in a country while knowing that they will not benefit the country's inhabitants in any way. For over ten years now he has been doing this research (guilt and money). According to his statements he has a file that may be worth a lot of money, he wonders? Maybe he will contact some contractors? Why? What might be the results? What are the risks?

In the next session, he is overcome by the medication and says that he is falling asleep increasingly often. I wonder if the antidepressant may be causing this excessive sleep. He reports a dream: *a figure is entering his bedroom like a shadow; he is afraid of it*. I invite him to talk about his fears as a child: he shared a bedroom with his brother but he does not want to go into this any further. At the end of the session, I wonder about his current state of health, since he does not talk about it any more.

The repressed unconscious mobilised by this long work gradually emerges; Damien talks about the fear of death and mentions that in the dream it is his bedroom, and the shadow represents the metastases. He talks about his dream and the black silhouette that he likens to his wife.

He mentions various fears he has had in the years since his childhood: drowning, an accident, his wife's "madnesses"—he relates a scene of marital violence in which his wife is chasing him with a knife in the kitchen. He thinks that "fear, either you feel it or you don't." He raises his voice a lot when he talks, as if the emotion were overwhelming him, as if also the aggressive drives were beginning to manifest themselves in our sessions. He mentions the thought of taking a mistress, but says no more about it.

Damien has stopped the antidepressants on my advice, having also obtained the psychiatrist's agreement; for a fortnight he has been experiencing an internal ferment. He talks about the physical relaxation of his body; his jaw is less tight, he is eating until he is full without any spasms, his abdominal muscles are now less tense, having been tense ever since the operation. I question why; what is he defending himself against? What is the threat?

The night before, he had a nightmare and his daughter, worried, came to see him in his bedroom to check that he was all right.

A new year begins; Damien reports various pieces of good news— no metastases in the liver, no more arterial tension, no more vertigo or headaches, no more antidepressants—no bad news. He emphasises how far he has progressed in his thinking and in his therapy.

He then tells me about the reasons for his marriage to his wife. He talks first about his time as a student in Paris where he lived alone and fell madly in love with a young woman who ultimately did not want to continue the relationship. He took this rejection very badly, alone in Paris, and still wonders today how he did not do anything stupid: "the pain was so strong." Damien then describes his involvement in the May '68 movement. After these events, he went on holiday with a friend and they met two young girls. Damien very much wanted to see one of them again and then had the idea of going off with her bicycle; in fact, the tactic worked—he saw her again and she became his wife.

It is at this time that his father died, and that his mother, who did not work, was forced to sell the family house; as a result of his father's death, his two youngest siblings, a brother and a sister, were unable to complete their studies. He links the choice of his wife to all these events; unlike his mother, she had an occupation. She had character, but not like his mother; he did not want to relive a romantic disappointment and he protected himself from this. She had a property inheritance that would have prevented the situation that his mother had experienced when his father died.

He then wonders about his choice of wife: why did he choose her? He mentions the huge urticaria that suddenly appeared on his wife's body the day before their wedding. Today, he associates this event with an unconscious rejection by his wife, who preferred tall, fair-haired men like her brother and one of his friends she went out with; they were not very serious-minded young men, unlike him, and physically he is short and dark-haired. He then associates about his wife's rages, if not mad episodes, and the impasse in which she has put him; on several occasions in the past, she has asked for a divorce, but he has always refused. He wonders in the session about the assault that his wife suffered, a real trauma that led her to leave Paris. He wonders about the reality of that assault; for her it was a big trauma, but did she tell him the truth—was it not a pretext for gaining some distance? Moving away from him?

He explains, at the beginning of another session, that his wife left him to live in the provinces at the end of the 1990s. He reports a dream:

> *He is in a cycling race squad; he sees he is at the back of the squad, and suddenly he breaks through and can overtake everyone. Then there is an*

> *accident, many people are injured, perhaps some technical staff who are accompanying the race. The dream then turns to a nightmare: some kinds of bizarre shapes arrive and throw themselves on the injured people. A lot of violence; he is surprised by this gratuitous violence.*

This dream is told following the account of his rivalry with his spouse's suitors, whom he met on cycle rides. In his nightmare, his aggressive impulses attack and he triumphs over his rivals. The narcissistic dimension of Damien's personality manifests itself in many aspects of his professional life; he wants to triumph at any cost in a grandiose way.

In our next session, Damien describes a situation he has experienced in the last few days: he feels hot and cold; his teeth are chattering.

I suggest that these are episodes of distress, but he does not associate; he relates a new dream: *he is talking with his son about the sale of the house in which the son is living.* The story of his son takes him back to his current worries—selling his house to carry out his projects. He returns to the previous session, where he had made reference to meeting a woman some years ago, when he "passed by another possible future," and he adds that he feels he has totally blocked himself: "I have nothing, I receive nothing. I don't know how to receive or take."

Damien tells me that his wife is threatening to kill herself and has said it would be his fault. He talks about his anxiety and a recently-published book about depression. "There are two types of worriers," he says, "the visible and the invisible." He returns to two of his character traits: "vigilant and over-active;" his statements lead him to talk very loudly and he states that he will not "give up this position like that," an allusion to his wife who makes him angry. He refers in this connection to the chivalric values that fascinate him: being dubbed by the overlord of the knights. He sees himself as a valiant knight.

At the next session, Damien states that when he left the previous session, he felt a strong emotion—some memories of the boarding school came back to him, and suddenly he says "you made me suffer, Daddy." Finally, the father appears, along with the psychological sufferings that this man imposed on him at an early age. I emphasise that the mourning has not yet been done. He replies that it is at the boarding school that he became hardened. He talks about his father and states that his "brothers are even angrier" than him. He remembers some presents his father gave him: a bicycle at the end of the last year of primary school, tickets to see the Globetrotters. When he was seventeen years old he insulted him, and from then on his father never embraced him again. "My father did not protect me, he was not a good overlord; he persecuted us all. I want to become a Knight," says Damien, talking very loudly and gesticulating with his hands. When his father died, he felt very empty inside.

I point out to him the aggression that is manifested towards his father, and I wonder out loud about possible wishes to see him disappear; I add that I can understand his feelings of guilt, because it is a long time ago now that his father died. Damien is moved, and feels sorry because he was not able to tell him that he loved him. His father was a very well-known man, and socially valued; he is proud of him.

It is now possible to understand Damien's efforts throughout his life: to overcome the trauma of the abandonment and to prove that he is a worthwhile person, hence the immense emptiness at his father's death. His father was not able to see his success.

Of the five children in his family, he is the only one to have had children; he remembers that his father helped him while being severe. He encouraged him to leave when he won his scholarship; moreover, he did not stop him from moving to Paris, instead he bought him a dinner jacket.

A childhood memory appears: as a small child he had insomnia, and he left his bedroom to go down to the living room on the floor below. His parents were dancing and he surprised them and then his father gave him "an enormous slap around the ears." As for his mother, she never comforted him in the various stages of his life.

Damien talks about emotions that overwhelm him and take him by surprise in the metro when he is listening to some music. Is it not a distant echo of his parents' dancing?

He is in a bungalow: on the ground floor, there is a fire; he does not know if he should run away, and he is told that it is very cold outside and that if he goes out he will be taking a risk.

This dream portrays his account of his childhood, but also the current experience of being emotionally overwhelmed—a resumption of psychic activity and the intrinsic fears in returning to the past.

Damien now talks about his grandfather, who died of anal cancer (not forgetting his own colorectal cancer); he wonders about the repetition of intergenerational events.[1]

He continues by returning to the different periods of his life. In his native town he was wonderfully happy, and he wishes to return there one day soon; after the events of May '68 and his father's death, he had had a difficult winter following an intense and disappointing romantic relationship: "that was a very difficult time." Three years later he got married.

He concludes that he lacked both maternal and paternal affection; he very quickly gave up expecting any affection from his mother. He expects nothing "from the other" emotionally and does not wish to get too involved himself. He also chose a wife who demands a lot of affection but gives very little—slightly in the maternal mode.

He then clearly mentions the nature of his conflict between a very demanding ego ideal that he attributes more to an identification with that of his father than his mother. It is the paternal ego ideal that has enabled him to confront involvements and responsibilities; his ego wishes to escape, explore the world, and travel. He has developed his professional involvement by also starting to work as a consultant five years ago, in connection with his new work in archaeological investigation. His desire is clearly focused on exploration and adventure. He tells me about his lassitude after twenty-five years in the business consultancy that diverted him from his early wishes. Towards the end of the session, as a return of the conflict with his father resurfaces in the transference, he confronts and contradicts me, in a real conflict of authority that I go on to interpret in the transference relationship, as if having evoked the entire account of his life, he remained on the oedipal positive side of "scores to be settled".

The year progresses. Following the last session, Damien worked at length (in self-analysis) on his ambivalence towards his father and his mother. He went back over what I had said to him, not about the current mother but the mother of his childhood; very often, patients want to resolve old childhood conflicts with the current parents and I draw their attention to the confusion of the problematics and the imagos.

He noticed that he did not have the same childhood memories as his brothers and sisters, and he finally realised that his problems arose in relation to his mother. At the end of the session, he returns to his father's death, over thirty years ago; since this time, he had only visited his father's grave once. He had noticed that his mother's attitude had changed profoundly since his death, as if for his mother it had been a relief, or as if she had thought "good riddance"; that is what he thinks.

This "good riddance" was the countertransference thought that had occupied me two weeks earlier, when I was infuriated by the length of the session and the overabundance of words that filled the space. Deep inside, I had asked myself in the countertransference relationship, "why this lassitude?" Damien thinks that his mother has been much happier since his father's death and he returns to a serious omission, which is that his father's tomb has never borne his name since his burial. He has reproached his mother about this, saying that she should have his father's name engraved on the tomb.

The psychotherapy progresses, and we have moved from somatic problems to the oedipal problematic in both its aspects: the negative side and the positive side. Next he returns to his childhood and the fact that, all the time he was at the boarding school between the ages of ten and fifteen, his mother had never written to him nor sent any parcels, whereas his father had visited him regularly. He remembers many details about his mother's behaviour towards his brothers and his sister; she was never kindly disposed towards them and always defended herself against their criticism by hiding behind their father's prohibition, as if she had had no autonomy to make decisions. Damien thinks that this was a piece of play-acting by his mother and that she never felt any tenderness or warmth towards her children.

Damien goes back to the progression of therapy in the October and November of the previous year, which gradually enabled him to talk in a more genuine way about what he deeply felt and his internal conflicts; he mentions an episode at that time of a very strong emotional discharge in a quarrel with his wife, in which he broke a door in his home with a poker. His wife told him at the time that it would be better if he sorted out his conflicts with his mother rather than with her. He mentions another incident, this time with his daughter in front of the television: taking advantage of one of his absences from the living room, his daughter had switched the television channel and, when he came back into the room, there was a violent quarrel with her, which ended in his daughter furiously switching off the television and leaving. Damien then picked up a stool with which he threatened his daughter.

I warn him very gently about this violence caused by narcissistic rage, so that he does not inadvertently injure those close to him. He must learn to be wary of himself and to withstand frustrations. I also acknowledge that the emotional discharge of the situations described has had some beneficial effects as well, but suggest that we might reflect together on whether there are other processes for avoiding such outbursts. After all, he destroyed a door and threatened his daughter. We part on these words, knowing that next time he will have to bring me his dream from the previous Saturday.

Damien relates that, in the twenty-four or forty-eight hours following the last session, he dreamt that:

> *Two men in a small housing estate are coming to visit a house; a woman greets them. They visit this house and Damien is particularly struck by two things: the living room is divided in two by a sort of veil, and a staircase leads down to a cellar at the exit from the last room. He tries to go down, and he has the sensation that he may fall and that if he does he is in danger of killing himself.*

In the session, Damien talks about a meeting with his brother who talked to him again about their father's violence towards their mother and towards them. He also remembers that his mother only wanted to have two children and that she had actually had five. This helps to explain the role of the death threat in the dream because the house partly represents the one in which he grew up, with its hidden staircase, and the death wishes he attributes to his mother.

He continues the analysis of his dreams: in a previous session he had had a dream with two houses. One was his father's and the other was his mother's. I had initially identified his mother's house with the human body:

> *Damien was entering this house and he came to a huge room with a large picture-window. This room was divided in two by a transparent curtain that went over the tables and chairs, marrying their shapes. On his left, there seemed to be an opening in the wall with a pillar to which he clung. He leaned over the void and felt a great fear of falling.* This dream specifies the description of the house and the veil that divides the room in two.

He continues to associate: reflecting on this, his mother's house refers to his mother's move after the family house was sold. She was then sixty-five to seventy years old, her age at the time of the first dream that he had reported; I had asked him at that time what had happened and he had not remembered. Today, he goes on to say that his mother had moved into the house next door (the veil of the first dream reappears here), in a flat that occupied two floors; the floors were connected by a staircase identical to that of his dream. As he was afraid that his mother might fall on the stairs, with his brothers and sisters he had installed a ramp made of some large rigging, such as is found on boats.

We can no longer continue analysing the previous dreams because Damien reports two new one that must all be interconnected by a common thought. In the first of his dreams:

He witnessed a quarrel between his elder brother and his younger brother. His younger brother is anti-establishment and slightly left-wing and his elder brother is more capitalist; in his dream he was trying to separate his two brothers who were arguing.

At the end of the session, he tells me about his current difficulties because he is afraid of having no money left to help both his son and his daughter. After several years away from his professional activity, he is reaching the end of his financial reserves; he has some important projects that he wants to carry out and he cannot allow himself to use this money to help his children. It should be noted here that his children are both adults, aged thirty and twenty-eight years; I point out to him that they are of an age to support themselves. I connect what he has told me at the end of the session with the dream in which he witnesses a family quarrel and likens this conflict to that which he is currently experiencing with his two children. Damien agrees with this, he likens his daughter to his younger brother and his son to his elder brother; he understands the nature of his dream and leaves me pensively.

Later, in another session, he returns to the dream about his mother's house, suggesting a possible interpretation connected with his mother's financial difficulties when his father died—she had no other solution than to sell this house to be able to continue to educate her children. Similarly, Damien today is obliged to choose between helping his children and carrying out his projects.

The psychotherapy has taken an increasingly psychoanalytic direction and Damien is becoming increasingly lucid; he relates a memory from over seven years ago that may enable him to understand his "vertigo spells". He was at his mother's house with his wife, and he suffered from vertigo during a conversation about his brothers and sisters and the desire for children in general. That must have awakened unconsciously the dangers hovering over his existence. He states that he believed he experienced that because, in looking at his spouse, he discerned some malice as if she too wanted to get rid of him. I think that what was probably a vasovagal episode was in fact a way to escape from a conflictual situation. He continues to talk about his close female relationships—with his daughter, mother, and mother-in-law—and recognises that he is turning the aggression against himself; he is too controlled in his relations with them.

I now understand better the possible aetiology of the illness. Following repeated daily conflicts with his spouse, and an assault that she suffered (a trauma for both of them), he relived some episodes from his childhood; not being wanted by his mother, being removed from the family home at the age of ten, and long years of solitude at an early age. He could no longer hold on to his wife, who wanted to move away from Paris and divorce him in the long-term; his life was falling apart, paving the way for severe illness by unbalancing the immune system. The cancer appeared after his second vasovagal episode and vertigo attacks that heralded a progressive slow somatic disorganisation between the systems.

"I've always felt I can deal with things alone, that I'm better than other people." Damien has difficulty asking for help and, nevertheless, he finally engaged in a therapy that was initially psychosomatic and then psychoanalytic, once the psychosomatic unity had been repaired.

The last few months of the therapy were devoted to his life plans with his wife: to rejoin her in the provinces, to live with her or in another flat—once again, the two houses reappear here. But Damien does not want to divorce, and he understands that the rapprochement is a source of conflict; he wants to maintain some distance but continue to see his wife. He therefore decides to rent a flat and to carry out his projects, and we part after many years of therapy. I am reassured about his psychic strength and the remission of the cancer.

APPENDIX TO THE CASE

Multimorbidity and integrative psychosomatics (Barnett et al., 2012; Salisbury, 2012; Roublev, 2012)

*Multimorbidity becomes the norm, in relation
to hyper-specialised medicine*

In an article of 14 May 2012, Dr Anastasia Roublev indicates the problems raised by multimorbidity in a world of highly-specialised medicine; in this respect, her article enables us to continue to reflect on the best way to address the problems of multimorbidity and the gaps in medical training, as it has been possible to study in the cases I am presenting here.

For logical, historical, practical and educational reasons, the teaching of medicine and continuing medical training are segmented by specialism and pathology. Similarly, the care of patients suffering from a grave illness, as outpatients and especially in hospital, is increasingly often carried out by specialists or hyper-specialists. Now, from experience, practitioners know that many patients suffer from more than one condition and that comorbidities often interfered with the diagnosis of the different pathologies and especially with the treatments of patients (Roublev, 2012).

A team of public health specialists in Glasgow and Dundee launched an epidemiological study across a broad spectrum that is representative of the Scottish population: data from the files of 314 medical centres, concerning 1,751,841 people—one third of the Scottish population—have served as a basis for this work. For each individual, their socio-economic level and the presence of forty "pathologies" were recorded, as well as the usual demographic data. There was, in fact, a set of well-determined conditions (such as hypertension or chronic obstructive bronchopneumopathy), sets of conditions (such as thyroid diseases or chronic inflammatory rheumatisms), syndromes (such as cardiac deficiency or kidney deficiency), or symptoms (such as chronic constipation or chronic pain, whatever its cause or its localisation) that are commonly encountered in general medical practice. Among this population, of all ages, 42.2 per cent of subjects demonstrated at least one of the forty pathologies, and 23.2 per cent a multimorbidity. The prevalence of multimorbidity was, of course, age-related, because, for example, between sixty-five and eighty-four years, 65 per cent of subjects suffered from at least two chronic pathologies, and over eighty-five years this prevalence reached 80 percent, with each subject then suffering from an average of 3.62 pathologies. However, although ageing is therefore a key factor in multimorbidity, in absolute terms the number of subjects affected by it was higher below the age of sixty-five years (210,500) than above (194,996). To a lesser degree, the socio-economic level also influenced the prevalence of multimorbidity, with 10 per cent of the population living in the poorest regions being affected in one case in four compared to one case in five for the 10 per cent living in the richest regions. As a result, multimorbidity appeared ten to fifteen years earlier in the 10 per cent of the poorest subjects than in the richest 10 per cent.

Finally, it emerged that a psychiatric morbidity was linked with a somatic morbidity in around one-third of the subjects affected by multimorbidity, with this type of comorbidity over-represented in women, and in the poorest subjects.

When a medical article or medical information refers to psychiatric and somatic comorbidity, it must be understood that this concerns the psychic apparatus; the ill subject reappears here and no longer the illness or illnesses.

> Altogether, if this study only confirms what everyone sensed (the fact that age and fragility are detrimental to health!), it has the advantage of shedding light on and specifying the major and probably growing importance of multimorbidities in medical practice. (Roublev, 2012)

This situation should perhaps lead to a reflection on both the initial and continuing training of doctors and the organisation of care, both for outpatients and those in hospital. The authors and the editorial writer of *The Lancet* (Roublev, 2012; Salisbury, 2012) outline some avenues in these areas. In the first, the training of practitioners, they think it would be desirable for the recommendations that increasingly underpin our practice to be adaptable in a simple way to the commonest comorbidities, perhaps when that is possible with the help of bespoke software programs. In the second area—the organisation of medical practice—they advocate bringing an end to the fragmentation of care by encouraging a grouping-together of multidisciplinary teams of health professionals in urban medical centres and in hospitals by increasing the role of general practitioners and internists in treating patients suffering from multimorbidities. Finally, they suggest it is essential, despite the difficulties, that major studies that establish the legitimacy of the recommendations should include, in future, subjects more representative of the real world; that is, in plain terms, more elderly or very elderly subjects and more patients suffering from multimorbidities. She adds that

> it remains to be seen whether such an endeavour to reverse the fragmentation of medical training and patient care is achievable in practice because of the strong established tendency to hyperspecialisation … . And if it is really desirable, to the extent that it may lead to a loss of efficiency with regard to the most serious conditions. (Roublev, 2012)

Will we ever emerge from the logic of specialisation and hyperspecialisation under the pretext of efficiency? It is not certain that efficiency is lost when we reintroduce the ill subject in his relationship with the illness; omitting the psychic apparatus from the assessment of patients' health and the aetiology of the illnesses is a major scientific gap, as will be noted with chronic illnesses and in autoimmune diseases and cardiac problems. The psychic apparatus would allow medicine to establish interconnections that it does not currently make between the subject's psychic experience (anamnesis), his family and professional environment, his behaviours, and his emotional life. It is impossible to treat patients while only considering biological variables. This fails to recognise the human dimension of patients.

CHAPTER FIVE

Lucien: type 2 diabetic; the patient's cultural dimension, denial of illness and narcissistic problematic

In 1996, a nurse from the endocrinology department who was interested in the psychosomatic approach that I was developing contributed strongly to directing me towards the study of certain pathologies. I first encountered the limitation of cardiovascular risk with a patient[1] suffering from a cardiac deficiency that required a transplant; he was living with a new heart and I wondered how he was finding the experience of his new life. It is at that time that I embarked on a long scientific investigation with my colleagues in the cardiology department, which enabled me to write my research study on transplants. I met nearly 200 patients who had undergone organ transplants over several years; later I will discuss the case of a transplant patient, Alicia, whom I will remember to the end of my days.

This nurse's other recommendation was to point me towards Professor André Grimaldi's diabetology department; he received me very kindly while encouraging me to observe the patients in his care. I took some of them into psychosomatic psychotherapy. I therefore divided my time between my patients who were suffering from cardiovascular problems following metabolic syndrome and my patients in the diabetology department. At the time of writing, I still share the medical and therapeutic preoccupations of my diabetologist colleagues who have allowed me to join in over the last twelve years with the reflections of a particular group called "the struggling diabetologists", a group in which we talk about the difficulties of treating some patients. We all explore together the various diagnostic elements, and I add to this the psychic dimension without which, for me and now for them, there would be no general approach to the patients. I have a great deal of esteem and consideration for these colleagues who have agreed to have a dialogue with me as we reflect together on the best care to provide to our patients in both the psychic and the medical dimensions. I think that this approach illustrates the potential of integrative psychosomatics in the hospital setting, and in the teaching at the Faculty of Medicine.

The first steps I took in the diabetology department led me to Lucien, who greeted me with a smile in his room in one of the wings in the department. He was listening to his radio; I think it was betting or lottery games but I did not hear any more because he quickly switched it off. As usual, I introduced myself as a psychosomatician who would supplement my departmental colleagues' medical approach by trying to establish some connections between the events in his life and the somatic problems for which he had been hospitalised. These might be current events, but also past events going back to his childhood. Patients understand this very well and start to tell their life histories.

I am often approached by psychology students from various departments of Paris University who want to undertake a clinical training, to which I sometimes agree. For the observation of this patient, I was accompanied by two of my students who silently attended the interviews and who, sometimes in my absence, observed patients while reporting the sessions to me in a clinical supervision. This is a university hospital and the patients willingly accept the presence of students, which sometimes brightens their day.

Before addressing Lucien's anamnesis and establishing all the connections between his life events, his psychic functioning, and his somatic problems, I would now like to present some theoretical clinical considerations concerning diabetic patients that I presented at a diabetology conference in 2003. This paper is entitled: "Non-observance and denial of illness; what are the psychological processes that generate resistance to treatment in high-risk diabetic patients?"

Confronted with the announcement of the diabetic illness, the psychological reaction of some patients is to protect what they believe to be their bodily integrity by setting up mental defences that put them beyond the reach of the treatments prescribed by the diabetologists. The object of my paper was to understand the nature of the psychic mechanisms that underlie these defensive behaviours, with a view to helping the doctors to treat their patients more effectively.

In the hospital departments, the diabetologists are confronted, in some patients, with problems accepting the illness and therefore observing the treatments, leading in the medium and long term to the emergence of major somatic disorganisations: retinopathy, nephropathy, cardiovascular problems, micro- and macro-angiopathies and so on, followed by attacks on the lower limbs (osteitises etc.). Our colleagues often note that in-patients end up controlling their diabetes until they leave the hospital departments; shortly afterwards, the hypoglycaemia cycles reappear twice to three times weekly, and the infernal cycle begins again with deteriorations in health. It is undeniable that, for most patients, the medical action on observance behaviours is effective and well-followed because the doctors represent a parental authority, but in many other cases all that can be seen is the medical powerlessness to protect patients when they do not observe their treatments.

I suggest a number of hypotheses to explain the denial of illness and resistance to observance. For many years, Professor Grimaldi has been encouraging me to practise the observation of non-compliant patients and to treat them in psychotherapy. I have not yet been able to carry out an epidemiological study; for the time being I am concerned with observations and clinical treatments.

I have noticed that when the illness has been diagnosed in childhood (between five and ten years of age), this acts as a brake on the psychosexual maturation process that has been interrupted by the diagnosis. For most of the patients I have observed since 1998, the mental genital organisation has not been established, and psychoaffective immaturity predominates in their behaviour, revealed by an incapacity to establish satisfactory adult relationships. For patients who discover their illness in adolescence or adulthood, a process of psychic regression takes place, leading to a reactivation of narcissistic defences.

With an injury to their narcissistic omnipotence, a characteristic of the early stage of mental life in which they have become stuck, the patients use archaic defence mechanisms, such as denial, to protect themselves from an intolerable and traumatic reality (mourning bodily integrity; mourning a somatic function). This fixation in a narcissistic position has caused a splitting of the personality (ego) between a part in which the patient lives his daily life while denying all the restrictions connected with the illness, and another part in which this continues to develop in the bodily domain. The splitting allows a fragile homeostasis, beyond which the destructive drive, which cannot be exercised outside the individual, continues to operate while progressively impairing the somatic functions. It is this de-fusion between the life drive and death drive that underlies the attack on the functions; deadly psychic processes are at work.

When the illness advances and the patients' bodies are visibly afflicted by problems such as osteitis, we see that, confronted with the impossible mourning for their lost health, they are willing to sacrifice the part for the whole and accept the suggested amputations. The physical pain replaces the psychological suffering. Prostheses often play the role of a rebalancing narcissistic object, much to the doctors' surprise. In all these cases, the amputation of an organ is experienced as safeguarding the narcissistic integrity.

Body psychotherapies allow a continuity to be restored between the body image and the psychic apparatus, with a view to reinforcing the psychosomatic continuity and overcoming the splitting processes. Short psychotherapies focused primarily on reinforcing behaviours and cognition can strengthen psychic structures impaired by illness by means of the psychotherapist's active and empathetic attitude. The objective here is to restore the capacity to observe the treatment via the long-term acceptance of the illness.

Lucien's somatic problems

Lucien has occupied a room in the department since mid-March; at the time of my consultation he is forty-seven years old. He has been hospitalised for an aggravated kidney deficiency and "Charcot's foot" in his left foot; he does not seem to realise the gravity of his condition, although the amputation of the foot and dialysis are in prospect. The only question he asks me is: "what type of shoes will I be able to wear after the operation?"[2]

Lucien states that he banged his foot last year and that when he pulled at the skin, it tore. The wound quickly became infected and he took himself to hospital. Then in December, an accumulation of blood appeared on the calf, and he could no longer walk; he shows me his leg at the same time.

Lucien is suffering from diabetic neuropathy, and it must be understood that when the nerve fibres of pain are affected and damaged, patients retain a sense of touch that enables them to feel the inside of their shoes when putting them on and taking them off. This gives them the illusion that their feet and body are complete, which can encourage them to take risks against the doctors' recommendations. The neuropathy *exacerbates the psychic blindness* to sensory perceptions; patients with a narcissistic organisation then perceive their omnipotence to be increased and take careless risks.

Lucien is being treated in hospital for suspected phlebitis; a few days later, he says: "the blood moved down to the level of the foot and some pus came out." He was treated for osteitis, and twenty days later he could walk again.

Lucien is married, and the father of five children; however, in other statements to young interns who have come to draw up the medical files, he stated that he had only one son. He had concealed the birth of his first four daughters. He has known his wife since he was seventeen years old; she is now living in French Guiana with her youngest son. His other sons (once again, a slip) live in France and do not visit him in hospital because they travel a lot.

His diabetes was discovered when he was forty years old and in hospital for an injury to the right foot; he had struck himself with a spade and this had led to his fifth right toe being amputated. Since then, he states, his diabetes has been stable.

While adding this information to what was provided to the doctors, I note that Lucien injured his foot with a pick-axe after he moved to French Guiana for his work, not long after his arrival from France. Already suffering from diabetic neuropathy, which he did not know, he did not notice that he was injured because he felt no pain; shortly afterwards, he experienced bouts of fever for which he was taken to hospital, where the wound to his right foot was discovered, leading to neuropathic ulceration as a secondary infection. The biological assessment identifies a glycaemia of 4.38g/l. The local evolution of the wound being unfavourable, the patient was sent for transmetatarsal amputation, then moved to the diabetology department. He is regularly monitored at the hospital and receives a complete assessment every year; he now also seems to have some nephrological problems. His left foot is hurting and he can no longer put his shoes on; he has had major weight fluctuations, ranging from 105kg to 80kg, with an increase to

87kg at present. He tells me that he is feeling better. As he expressed it, he is going to have a fistula installed if a dialysis proves necessary, but not for a year. The next amputation operation "bothers" him, but he is not having specific dreams; "maybe some small nightmares." He had a headache after he was moved to the nephrology department, but he is not suffering from migraines. According to my interpretation, this symptom emerged to inhibit the frightening thoughts about the amputation (and therefore the reactivation of castration anxieties). We know that the migraine is there to impede thinking; it was a way for Lucien to forget about the dialysis, which he hates.

Lucien's history

Lucien's parents live in French Guiana; his father is now seventy-five years old and his mother is sixty-nine. One of four siblings, he has two sisters and a brother. No one in his family has diabetes. He does not follow a particular diet. He likes playing football; he was the trainer of a team but has not been able to do this for a year. However, he still goes hunting with friends, and sea fishing with his son; he has done a lot of walking in the woods and he wonders if he is still going to be able to go fishing.

Gradually, in the course of our conversation, Lucien's original identity emerges in the background, which I make a note to explore further so as to understand my patient better. Cultural identity is fundamental to understanding every aspect of a human being, and I faintly sense that Lucien has a fascinating cultural past that is worth knowing about. When Lucien talks about hunting and fishing, he does not talk in the same way as a French person who hunts or fishes; how is it different? This is one line of enquiry in the anamnestic investigation.

Lucien continues to describe the attacks on his body: he explains that his ankle is dislocated—his foot has become detached from the ankle and: "it just needs to be put back in place very tightly, then fixed with a metal plate to hold it all together." His explanation of a robotic body, in which bones are finally replaced by metal plates, like a machine, intrigues me, and I wonder very much about Lucien's image of his body.

He wonders how he can find out whether he will be able to go fishing with the prosthesis, because he is worried about what his eight-year-old son will think. Will he be able to put on his shoes; will he have a limp? He must be operated on the following week. In the silence of my thinking throughout our discussion, I wonder about the anxiety about the amputation that he has been able to create in me in the countertransference relationship—but where has *his* anxiety gone?

We continue by evoking his memories of childhood, and Lucien states that he does not think about it; he spent a happy childhood with his maternal grandmother and, as there was no school in the village where his parents lived, he went to live with his grandmother from the age of four until seven. Then he went to his uncle for three years, because his parents had moved to the vast Maroni River. His grandmother died when he was thirteen years old; he thinks that he was not a spoilt child, although he was often alone in his childhood. He had no dreams for the future, as he did not know what his future would be.

He went hunting and fishing from a very early age. He wanted to become a car mechanic, and did some studying and obtained his certificate. He first worked in a large mechanics company for two years, then he enlisted in the army, and as the pay was not very good, he applied to work in social services when he was twenty-three years old. He went through every stage at the social services, from accommodation to catering, admissions, emergencies, the surgical unit, and intensive care; he is now a nursing auxiliary, and for three years has been working in a less tiring role in the gerontology department because of his illness.

Gradually a very different man appears from the person lying in his bed, waiting for his foot to be amputated; I have before me a descendant of the hunter-gatherers of the Amazon jungle, a distant heir of our Neolithic ancestors. Culturally, of course, he is French, but it is important not to neglect his other cultural components and his original identity that form the whole of what I call the core of the self in the psychosomatic unity. Lucien is a hybrid of the Amazon jungle; what might his original name be?

The two female students who have accompanied me for the interview tell me about their observations: they think that Lucien seems to talk about his medical problems without being affected by them, with a certain detachment; he does not seem to be aware of the real consequences of the operations that are to be performed, in particular the amputation. All the patient's worries are centred on recovering his capacity to walk properly and put his shoes on; he is also very worried about how his son perceives his motor capacities. They note that Lucien tells his story very mechanically, as if learnt by rote, with no real participation or personal involvement. The events are lined up one after the other in an unconnected way. However, he is enthused by some subjects—such as his son and mechanics.

Initial commentaries: what is the role of the culture of origin?

The following commentaries arise from my interview with my two students. Lucien has strongly cathected his son and his work; I wonder if his son may in fact represent his double. His statements initially appear topical and factual, as with many somatic patients; likewise with his emotions, which he keeps at a distance. We ask ourselves some questions about the body image, as if Lucien were separated from his body or lives in a mechanical body with parts that can be changed at will. He does not worry, but his lack of worry creates some anxiety in me in the countertransference relationship. Lucien has strongly cathected movement and the release of tensions in his behaviour; he seems mainly to be worried about the image that he will present to his son after the operation. There are two ways of interpreting his worry: either he does not want to show his son that the amputation of his foot has deeply transformed his bodily integrity, or he is worrying, in the Wayampi cultural part of his psyche, about not being able to wander with him in the ancestral forest.

With patients who have complex cultural components, I adopted the habit, more than twenty years ago now, of giving interpretations according to both French culture and their culture of origin. We must understand that we can find ourselves dealing with cultural conflict inside the patient's psyche, but also cultural misunderstanding— I would even say cultural blindness—on the European psychotherapist's part. My patient Nina, whose case I set out in *When the Body Displaces the Mind*, had this double cultural component in her psyche. The medical director of the Institute of Psychosomatics, who had referred her to me having made a psychosomatic diagnosis, thought that Nina had an extremely impoverished imagination; after several years of therapeutic work, I was able to access, thanks to her trust, the part of her preconscious that she had carefully avoided revealing. This cultural part belonging to her community of origin had very important imaginative dimensions. This clinical experience, followed by many others since then, enabled me to think differently about patients with several cultural components; probable poverty in the French language, but a rich imagination in the cultural component of origin.

Another problem arose: Lucien's distancing of his emotions. As seen above, with my students who thought that Lucien did not experience his affects, it was briefly possible to put forward the hypothesis of either emotional suppression or alexithymic manifestations. When Lucien talks about his grandmother, he does not seem affected by her death. He tells us about her life in a very factual way, and mentions few memories. He has no dreams and associates very little, even on subjects that interest him; time seems to be abolished, but for this component I think that it is not Western time but Amazonian time. He was separated from this mother and father in early childhood and this raises a question about the introjection of the maternal object. He was fed but perhaps not "loved enough". He then established himself in a narcissistically omnipotent universe in which others, especially his son, are merely an extension of himself. There seem to be some natural forces nestling deep in his unconscious that give him great vitality and fuel his narcissism. I also ask myself some questions about the invisible entities that he does not dare to talk to us about; here I am referring to what in ethnopsychoanalysis we call "the invisible beings"—daemons, djinns, creatures of the forests, rivers, and lakes, and so on.

Our discussions continue

Lucien has just returned to his room after the amputation of his left foot; he does not seem to be suffering, probably because of the analgesics—there is no psychic suffering, and no anxiety. He has had a very positive experience of his operation, without any dreams or nightmares. His son and his wife have come to see him; he has said nothing to his son and has hidden his foot during the visit. He wishes to tell him nothing about the amputation until he has fully recovered, with the prosthesis firmly in place. He also wishes to have a course of physiotherapy to be able to control it completely. This seems to be his main concern, and without any emotion he remembers having seen a man with his foot amputated when he was thirty-two years old.

At a review meeting, I meet with my two students again to reflect on Lucien's situation. The fact that he is not dreaming confirms my initial hypotheses about what Marty calls the "density of the preconscious". Is his son the mirror of himself? Does he see himself through his son's eyes? Is his son the extension of himself? Does he see himself as a father wanting to transmit his ancestors' heritage to his son? I ask my students to reflect further on Lucien's ancestral beliefs and his relationship with his son.

Short commentary on life events in relation to the diabetes.

I go back over Lucien's history. Everything began after his move to French Guiana; it was only six months later that his wife joined him there. It seems that his wife plays the role of a maternal protective shield, and that her remoteness was a very bad experience for him. That might have led to a progressive disorganisation following a probable parapraxis; namely the unfortunate blow from the pick-axe. The identification with his son and his separation from him when he returned to French Guiana may have reactivated his painful separation from his parents in his past. Just before he was eight years old—his son's current age—he was handed over to his uncle; this involves a traumatic history of separation from his parents.

I also think that resituating the patient in his cultural context might make it easier to understand his behaviour and his psychic functioning. What is the human being's place in nature and in the universe in French Guiana? What are the Wayampi people's beliefs? How do these beliefs structure my patient's psyche?

My students put forward some interesting hypotheses of their own, reflecting the European view of other civilisations: how is the human being situated in the French Guianan universe? How is an individual defined in this society? Do the concepts of body and soul exist? Given that Lucien does not seem bothered by the amputation of his foot once it can be replaced by a prosthesis, might it not be thought that the body and its image have little importance for French Guianans, as long as the function is maintained or artificially reproduced? How are the transgenerational bonds formed? By what rituals?

I decide to continue the investigation of my patient.

The universe of the Amazonian forest

When I enter his room, Lucien is immersed in a Parisian weekly entertainment magazine: *L'officiel des spectacles*. I want to know a bit more about his native country; he seems distant, and goes on leafing through this magazine as he talks to me. He begins by describing the many types of fishing that he does in rivers or coves; he seems to have a vast knowledge of all the fish that he catches and how to cook them immediately on the beach. Then he begins to describe hunting. He lists the many animals that are hunted with guns: woodcocks, monkeys, caymans, pink flamingos, agoutis, parrots, porcupines, and so on. It was his grandfather who taught him these hunting and fishing techniques. Lucien is now teaching his son to fish and hunt; he therefore needs to be able to walk as soon as possible with his prosthesis: "I am trying to heal as fast as possible so I can go back there." Lucien is a different person when he describes his life as a hunter in the forest and he becomes his people's son again; he ceases to be the nursing auxiliary who works in France and speaks French. He is now teaching his son all the techniques, which explains why it is so important to be able to walk with his prosthesis. He wants to heal as quickly as possible to be able to return to the forest with his son; he comes to life tremendously when he talks about all his activities—affect reappears.

I usually ask patients about their spiritual beliefs to assess the possible recourses in the case of distress. Lucien tells me that he is a believer and shows me the Bible on the bedside table. He was brought up in a Catholic family, was christened, and has taken his first communion. However, he has not planned anything for his son, whose name I was never to know, whom he "leaves free to choose." He now talks about his four daughters; the eldest is twenty-eight, and the youngest is twenty-two years old. They live in metropolitan France and come to see him in hospital when they can. He is very reticent in talking about his daughters, revealing the woman's traditional place in his society of origin. His wife recently came with her son, but they left again because she had to return to work. How does he explain the age differences between all his children? It is nearly nine years since he and his wife had returned to French Guiana for a holiday, where they discovered that his wife was four months pregnant; he said that the scan showed it was a boy and they kept this.

How did he experience the separation from his wife for several years, while he was in France and she was in French Guiana? For nearly three years, he travelled back and forth, but he makes a mistake about the dates and his confusion finally annoys him. I think to myself that he has experienced this whole period as an abandonment, because his wife serves as an external object, on which he leans to live his life with the least possible excitation. This absence made him unconsciously relive the whole period of abandonment in the early period of his life, which aggravated the somatic problems.

Our interview causes him a lot of excitations, and to reduce these, Lucien talks about French Guiana again, describing its forest in poetic terms: "when day closes," he says, "the forest darkens while there is still some sun above the trees;" as if this forest were a sanctuary, a big garden in which he regains his inner calm. He follows the pathways and gets back in touch with nature. It seems that this forest is also the garden of his childhood; a secret garden that he has long explored and which in my opinion constitutes an internal universe-object, a recourse that enables him to survive. But this object is not adequate to ensure his daily equilibrium, unless he goes there every day.

On the day of our next meeting, when I reach the first floor in the building of the diabetology department, I meet Lucien near the lift, sitting in a wheelchair, smoking a cigarette. We go to his room to talk like old friends, which I find is the most appropriate and emotionally close form of relationship with our patients so that they understand that we are taking into consideration all the dimensions of their personality. I have to say that, in time, we end up becoming emotionally attached to our patients.

Lucien talks to me about his foot and shows me his stump so that I can see for myself how well the scar has healed. He is very happy because his knee bends easily, without any problem, and he demonstrates this to me by flexing it several times. He tells me that he will soon leave the diabetology department to go to the physiotherapy centre, so that an imprint can be taken to make his future prosthesis. He thinks he will return home next June; he is impatiently waiting "to go fishing and hunting."

He remembers that with his right foot, which is already semi-amputated, he could play football easily and without limping—"no one could tell," he says. "With good physiotherapy, everything should go really well." He remains convinced that he will make a full recovery, as if the current of narcissistic omnipotence had suddenly returned after his amputation. He no longer seems to be in denial, and I think about this specific feature of mammals that can amputate one of their paws to save the whole body. Is it the same for us human beings? This is a mystery of narcissism, and in this case we are perhaps no longer dealing with denial, as a certain bodily integrity had been restored.[3]

Lucien now talks to me about his son, whom he loves to take hunting and fishing; he bought him his first fishing line when he was five years old, and a second one more recently. He reports that the first time he went fishing, he caught a fish that weighed seven kilos, and he himself had difficulty pulling it out of the water because at that time his foot was already hurting him. His son loves fishing now; he also goes hunting with him, "but only hunting along known paths and roads." I understand from these words the danger of straying far from the roads and pathways. "There we hunt green parrots, macaws ... that we eat with vegetables, in a stew for example." Lucien loves cooking after having hunted. Since the earliest interviews, he has talked about how food is cooked, which is clearly very important to him. Gradually, we become aware of this man's life in his environment, and his particular way of getting back in touch with nature, animals, and the supernatural beings about which he never talks, except in relation to protective rituals, for example when with his son he does not want to stray far from the forest paths—moving away may put them at the mercy of these supernatural beings. Lucien has given his son a rifle with lead shot to "train himself to shoot at small birds." That reminds him of the hunting and fishing that he practised with his Wayampi maternal grandfather; his grandmother had the same origin. His grandfather had died at the age of eighty-five, which is seven or eight years ago now. He did not know his paternal grandparents, who were of Brazilian origin. He goes back over his past gradually and talks about his parents, who lived in a small village far from the town; his father was a meteorological engineer. He was brought up by his maternal grandparents, who regularly took him hunting and fishing; they taught him everything, transmitting the Wayampi culture to him.

Lucien now remembers his earliest working years: he worked from 9 o'clock at night to 8 o'clock in the morning. In metropolitan France, he worked in this way for twelve years, then he was transferred to French Guiana to the same type of post, and this situation suited him perfectly because he could go hunting and fishing during the day. He explains, as we will see later, his world view: "It is about fishing not to kill but to eat." His son gets back from school at four o'clock in the afternoon, and when he has done his homework they go out in all weathers, even if it is raining, because they are well-equipped.

As I had found him near the lift in his wheelchair, Lucien explains that he has returned to his room to wait for the doctor's visit but that he will be going for a walk immediately afterwards because he cannot bear to stay lying down in his room without moving. I think that his need for movement reveals that his body has recovered from the operation and that he will soon be ready to leave us.

The Wayampi world view

Before continuing, it will be helpful to explore the Wayampi world view to resituate Lucien in his universe of reference, because it is difficult to understand a human being's psychic functioning when he is severed from his cultural environment.

For the Wayampi, the universe is the work of creator gods who live in the sky, while the forest is the realm of the spirits; the rivers and marshes harbour supernatural beings. The symbolic arrangement of these spirits in space allows the sacred spatial zones to be demarcated from the profane regions. For tropical forest societies such as the Wayampi, it is mainly hunting and fishing that are accompanied by rituals. There are few sacred sites or places of worship in forests; this society believes in a global balance between natural resources, supernatural forces, and human beings, and the supernatural forces foster human activities by giving them natural resources, animals, and plants. In counterpart, as we have seen with Lucien, human beings adopt a rule of conduct not to abuse the resources of nature. Illnesses and death are always attributed to supernatural forces and considered as consequences of imbalances between human beings, natural resources, and spirits. Considerate behaviour towards animals will enable human beings to avoid illness and misfortune; immoderate behaviour will cause a conflict with the spirits, who are the masters of the animals.

I will never know how Lucien caused the imbalance that gave rise to his illness; it is important to examine how the beliefs constitute unconscious and conscious mental representations that structure the psyche, affects, and behaviours. Although he belongs to the third generation, Lucien continues to follow his ancestors' customs; in the constitution of his identity he has kept many beliefs, and many of his current behaviours are to be connected with his beliefs. As for every Wayampi, success in life is translated by the fundamental principle: "with my game and my fish, my wife can provide collective meals to my friends and to my relatives; with my wife's manioc beer, I can provide a party to the community." In this society, it is prestigious to display your knowledge by naming a large number of animal and vegetable species; we now understand why Lucien demonstrated his knowledge during our interviews. It was a way of showing himself to best advantage with my students and myself; provided, of course, that we understood the underlying reason for his statements. A European may overlook such utterances unless he is aware that this man, who has emerged from the Amazon forest of his ancestors, is communicating to us the essential components of his identity. In Wayampi society, initiation is the same for everyone: it must be *observed*. The father shows his son the plants, animals, and birds in the forest, and everything that can be of direct use in this context, accompanied by warnings to protect the life of human beings. Lucien was initiated by his grandfather; he wants to initiate his son in his turn, and we can easily understand that he wants to be physically able to take his son into the forest or to fish.

Example of the comprehensive learning approach based on observation

>A father and his son have gone into the forest to hunt, and come to a Guarea kunthiana tree bearing fruit.
>
>>The father: This is a ya t oa'ï, my son.
>>
>>The son: Yes, it is an old ya t oa'ï plant.
>>
>>The father: There are two young ones next to it, and germination clusters too.
>>
>>The son: The biggest is covered with ripe fruits.
>>
>>The father: It's fruiting late this year. Toucans love these fruits, you know. Since the other fruits liked by the toucans—
>>
>>The son: Like for example the kwa po'i fruit, the kunawalu'ï fruit, or the wasey palm fruit?
>>
>>The father: Yes, because those have already fallen, it is this tree we have to look for at the end of the season; we can be sure to find groups of toucans there. We shall have good toucan hunts
>
>The father looks for a fruit on the ground, gives it to his son who takes it in his hand, looks at it for a while, then throws it away: the lesson is over.
>
>Such an approach in learning applies to all fields of knowledge and starts as soon as a child is able to speak. From the canoe

> seat, mothers identify edible fruits growing on the river banks or name the different species of swallows skimming over the river. Undoubtedly the child's understanding will be long-lasting. From a very early age, he or she will be able to distinguish thousands of life forms and subtle differences in the surrounding plant world, while an ordinary Westerner will only see *an* indistinct vegetation mass. (Grenand & Grenand, 1996, pp. 187–188)

In this society, there is a constant atmosphere of competition and emulation; the men compete in their hunting and fishing and the women compete in relation to the culinary arts and the variety of food preparations. We can now understand what Lucien said about fishing, hunting, and food preparation, which constitute the essentials of life for the Wayampi, along with their spiritual practices; contrary to the hasty psychosomatic interpretations concerning words considered as factual and topical, this concerns the spirituality and symbolism of daily life. The use of natural resources in this society is totally codified because they only take what is necessary: "I eat a lot thanks to the big species; I eat every day thanks to the small ones." Lucien hunts "not to kill but to eat." Although the Wayampi have become partly sedentary, they have kept their capacity for mobility, which is strongly cathected and inherited from their distant Neolithic ancestors. We should not forget that Lucien cannot stay still for long; how then can his movement and behaviour be interpreted in psychosomatic terms, since this forms part of the Wayampi way of being in the world?

I will address the beliefs later to pursue the understanding and elaboration of this particular case.

The notes made by the nurses

In our diabetology department, the nurses also like to keep notebooks for their observations; the following notes were made twenty days after his amputation:

> *Abdominal pains at night; the next day, the patient is very edgy and has eaten very little; the following day the patient complains that everything is going badly; he is suffering from lumbar pains at night that require analgesics, he seems sad; the pains increase and he has to take codeine. The placement of the fistula for the dialysis seems to be greatly upsetting him.*

Suddenly the body reappears and the harsh reality dawns on Lucien.

At my visit to Lucien, when I enter the room, he is watching television and examining a chart of numbers, probably lottery numbers. We continue to talk about the forest and hunting so that I can learn a bit more about it. His grandfather would hunt alone at the roadsides; it is very dangerous to enter the forest and it takes several people to fathom it. In case of an accident, it must be possible to inform the rescue services. This is why he does not take his son into the forest, because it requires leaving for several days and sleeping in a hammock there. He describes a wild boar hunt that requires several hunters, because the animals are so heavy that only two can be brought back per person. The animals are drawn there and the livers are grilled and eaten. It is in fact his grandfather rather than his maternal uncle who initiated him into hunting, as has been seen above; he has hunted for a very long time and a few years ago he received a gun.

What were the emotional repercussions of his grandfather's death? How did he mourn this person he loved? Did the mourning have some implications for the diabetes? Lucien does not seem to be visibly affected by his grandfather's "departure", despite having lived with him for a great many years as a child and adolescent. His loss may have made silent inroads and caused major imbalances; this is a hypothesis to consider. His emotional distance from the events continues, as if to avoid showing the suffering of his soul.

Lucien is happy with the surgery on his foot, but expresses his great disappointment at having to undergo dialysis. This dependence on machines troubles him; he did not think he would have to have dialysis now, and he thought this solution would be later. He even hoped to avoid it by taking good care of his health when he went back to French Guiana; he thought simply that the placement of the fistula was preventive. He now realises how restrictive it may be, and he sees possible repercussions on his daily life, especially his hunting and fishing. He also knows that the dialysis would prevent him from going abroad because he intends to visit some neighbouring countries of French Guiana. This troubles him deeply because he likes travelling and moving around. I now also know that the Wayampi life is about travelling and mobility; it can therefore be said that we are witnessing a prevalence of behaviours because it involves their daily life, accompanied by symbolic processes and sensory daydreams. For the time being, Lucien will continue to work in the post that he currently holds.

My two students reflect on Lucien's future, because he has complained to his wife that everything is going badly; they wonder how they can tell how he will develop. Will he become aware of his condition and avoid playing football, for example, or will his condition deteriorate because his favourite activities are going to be restricted?

My clinical experience to date, with many patients who belong to very different cultures has, shown me that none of them talks spontaneously about beliefs that he knows perfectly well are not accepted by Europeans. This is an area in which communication is very difficult, unless we seek it out by telling our patients that we understand and accept them as they are without making any judgement. Lucien gave us a great deal of information about his life and his world view, as we have seen above. He talked about his mobility, the forest, his knowledge of plants, all kinds of animals, hunting and fishing, and the culinary preparation of the animals killed; without talking about supernatural beings, he alluded to them by means of prohibition, hiding many rituals intended to appease the invisible spirits in order to enter the forest. It is enough simply to listen and to accept, at a deep level, what the patient says.

My last meeting

When I arrive at the department, I find Lucien in the corridor; he explains to me that he is restless because the doctor is about to come round and he is waiting for him impatiently. In the last few days, he says, he has gone down into the small garden, in the sun, even if the weather was not very good, because as the place is sheltered it is very nice to spend some time there. He was actually wearing a tee-shirt there; he is not afraid of the cool weather because he has lived in Paris for over twenty-three years. In any case, he does not like staying in his room.

He will soon be leaving our department to go to the physiotherapy centre, where he will be able to try out his prosthesis and begin to walk. He hopes that there will be no delay, because he is impatient to return to his country. He talked to his son on the phone the previous day and, as soon as he returns, they will go fishing together. He will not be tired by the time difference because he will have slept on the plane. He will take advantage of his son's school holidays to take him into the forest and return to work in September, perhaps even in mid-August. Today, Lucien does not want our interview to end; he is very talkative, as if overwhelmed by the excitement of his imminent departure. He tells me how worried he is about the dialyses; he had his first dialysis this week and this is greatly upsetting him. He did not think he would have to have dialysis because he is urinating correctly, and also because he is "too young for that." He cannot do anything during the dialysis, with big tubes coming out of his arm and running over him to be connected with the machine. He has his little radio of course, but he cannot do anything because one of his arms is immobilised. It takes three-and-a-half hours, and he estimates that for the time being it is a long but acceptable period of time. However, he certainly cannot see himself doing this three times a week, and for four or five hours at a time; at most, he would be able to accept two a week but no more. He repeats this statement several times, as if to convince me and, above all, to convince himself. But what is this really about? Once again, the reality of the body is being manifested and suddenly imposed on the patient, who deeply rejects all constraints relating to the body. He adds that he does not see why three dialyses a week should be necessary when he is urinating correctly; throughout the last dialysis, he had a strange sensation of water flowing in his ears, which had never happened before (auditory hallucination). Since then, the impression has persisted and it disturbs him, but he has not talked about it to the doctor yet. He cannot bear the frustrations of a reality that imposes itself, and as if to reinforce his rejecting attitude to the dialysis, he repeats several times: "I don't want more than two dialyses, I will not accept a third; I would rather run away." He remains silent for several minutes. This is the first time since our conversations began that affect has appeared in his behaviour and in his words; he seems more human, less defensive, and more regressed, displaying an anxiety.

Lucien then returns, following a self-calming procedure of his own, to the forest that is his favourite environment in his imagination; he will hunt there, as usual, at the roadsides, but his son will not enter the big forest and he will wait until he is twelve years old. At that age, a child is capable of being very alert to what is happening on the ground, as it is necessary to pay constant attention to snakes that bite your hand as soon as you lower it. It is also necessary to be well-versed in the techniques for finding your bearings because you very quickly get lost in the forest. You need to know the landmarks since some trees grow close to the roads, which tells you where you are. You must also know that the small streams flow out into rivers and that if you follow the course of the river you can get out of the forest. He continues talking about all the techniques for entering the forest, leaving landmarks by breaking or cutting tree branches in order to find the way back. He continues to describe the trees, their names, their leaves, and so on. Today, Lucien does not accept that the interview is being brought to an end; he is taking me into the forest with him and does not want to be separated from me. I understand that he is clinging to our relationship following the ordeal that he has just undergone, which has caused him great anxiety; he is also thinking about our imminent separation. Talking about the forest has gradually reassured Lucien, revealing the mentalisation process used to strengthen himself narcissistically, to be reassured, and obtain inner calm; he is returning to the ancestral forest and assuming his place in the generational chain.

Reflections and commentaries

Throughout the interviews, many thoughts went through my mind in trying to understand Lucien. His remote attitude, lack of emotional expression, difficulty in giving any continuity to his life history, the factual and topical statements about his life events, and his robotic appearance when he was talking about his amputation and his future prosthesis all encouraged me to consider my patient's narcissistic dimension, since he was almost an operative patient.

To confirm my theoretical proposition, I was able to refer to the history of his early life in which the maternal absence, akin to what Green calls "the dead mother" (2001), confirmed my hypothesis that the object had not been introjected in the classical sense. I prefer here to refer to Kohut's approach, who prefers to use the term self-object, which implies an internal union between the self and the object, united in an undifferentiated way before the process of the separation of self and object.

I think the fact that Lucien was brought up by his grandmother in the early years of life, far away from his family, constituted a traumatic stage of his development, weakening the development of his immune system and forcing him, for the sake of emotional survival, to withdraw into the "narcissistic citadel"; I am forming the hypothesis of an emotional deficiency in the grandmother.

I must also reintroduce all the elements that gradually appeared during our interviews, specifically the Wayampi culture. Everything that Lucien told me was initially intended to show himself to me to best advantage in a sort of narcissistic exhibitionism; but, at the same time, he revealed himself as the son of his people, although he belongs to the third generation of sedentary people who have left the forest and therefore the Wayampi tribes. He had in another part of himself, of his ego, a world of resources that had enabled him to survive for a very long time. Gradually, I understood that the Amazonian forest represented a nurturing mother, the mother of the origins to which he was attached. In a certain way, Lucien was not alone inside; he had a symbolic, mythical, archaic object. It can then be understood that his arrival in France had severed him from his roots and that this was a genuine trauma involving the loss and abandonment of the mythical maternal roots. In coming to France he had also relived the maternal abandonment of his earliest years of life, the privation of the object's love, and the rescuing narcissistic retreat that ensued from this. He had temporarily lost the maternal forest.

We must also go back to the original discovery of the diabetes, which was when he was thirty-nine years old, following an unfortunate blow from a pick-axe that caused what is termed "neuropathic ulceration". His hospitalisation revealed his diabetes, but also neuropathic problems, arterial hypertension, and dyslipidaemia. These problems cannot emerge in a short space of time, which takes the medical hypotheses back to ten or fifteen years, when Lucien was twenty-four years old. It was at this age that he had left French Guiana to come and work in France as a nursing auxiliary.

In *Life Narcissism, Death Narcissism*, Green very pertinently develops the theory of narcissism: "narcissistic withdrawal does not call for any particular commentary, except that one must always remember that it is the response to suffering, to a sense of ill-being" (2001, p. 17). We are confronted with two configurations—primary narcissism and primary object love. For Lucien, the object has not become detached from the self, and the narcissistic withdrawal has occurred in a grandiose relationship to the maternal forest. This is a grandiose object allied to the grandiose self; as so well expressed by Green: "the object is, therefore, both there and not there at the same time" (ibid., p. 18). There is therefore no basis for denying the existence of primary narcissism in favour of primary object love; these are two complementary visions taken from different viewpoints.

* * *

Mary Fleury's excellent article (1999)[4] describes how names are given by the Wayampi people, which will explain why Lucien never told me his name:

There are various types of names for referring to human beings, according to the circumstances. So an individual has the following:

- a birth name, traditionally given according to the day of birth (although this custom of African origin is beginning to be abandoned), or according to the place in the family or the birth of twins. It is a name known only to those close to him and that is extremely significant from the cultural viewpoint.
- he also has one (or several) familiar surname(s) in everyday life that can refer to a childhood event or a characteristic of the individual; thus one child was called *komukomu* (cucumber) in memory of an impressive number of cucumbers eaten.
- finally he has an official name, corresponding to the civil status, which appears on identity papers and is given to strangers and used at school and in administrative procedures.

A connection can therefore be made between the individual's birth name and the ritual name of the plant, between his familiar name and the name that denotes a characteristic of the plant, and finally between the official name and the one that refers to the classification. A parallel can therefore be drawn between the nomenclature system for vegetables and that for human beings. This system also corresponds to a pronounced predilection for secrecy among the Maroon Blacks. In fact, the existence of several names makes it possible to refer to a person or a plant in front of a third person without that person being able to identify who is being talked about unless he or she knows the synonyms used.

However, the various names used do not all have equivalent status: the ritual name of the plant has a certain intrinsic power because it must be uttered only in certain circumstances, and an individual's birth name is known by very few people (in fact, *kali nem* "calling the name" means "putting a curse"). This demonstrates the full importance of the name, whether it is for human beings or plants and vegetables. If the name, as Levi-Strauss (1962) states, is *a linguistic sign situated halfway between percepts and concepts, like the elements of mythical thought*, we see that there is a spectrum on which the different names are situated; the secret, intimate name, whether it is that of the individual or the plant, is the closest to the concept, unlike the official name or classificatory name that seems the most remote.

CHAPTER SIX

Alicia: "when I've had the transplant, will I feel better?"

Alicia is a remarkable woman, with a strange and moving destiny. Her capacity to deal with the most terrible ordeals is awe-inspiring. Her extraordinary lucidity about her life and her associative capacities suggested to me that she had already done some psychotherapeutic work, which turned out to be the case when she told me about this during the interview. Alicia is the patient with whom I have had the most dialogue during my research into transplant patients.

Alicia is a woman of around fifty years, who has recently had a kidney and pancreas transplant. When the doctor asked her if she would be willing to talk to a psychosomatician, she immediately agreed. I therefore show my new patient to the office that I am kindly being lent; it is located on the first floor of the building that houses the kidney-pancreas transplant unit. I notice that Alicia has some difficulty climbing the stairs, and we exchange some words with a view to establishing a relationship; it is not easy to talk about oneself immediately.

Crucial questions in any psychosomatic interview are how to approach the other, what mental and emotional distance to keep, and how to establish a relationship of trust.

We are talking like old friends after a few minutes, which confirms my intuition of a previous therapeutic relationship. Alicia addresses the relations between doctor and patient because she has long and difficult experience in this subject. She thinks that doctors should listen to their patients more; she also complains about psychologists' or psychiatrists' lack of information relating to transplants and the difficulty of conversing with them.

Alicia's complaints

"The kidney–pancreas transplant is no picnic," says Alicia, remembering her recent trials. Confronted with symptoms that they cannot explain, doctors say that it is psychosomatic: "it's all in the mind … when they don't know, doctors blame the patients." Alicia seems particularly unhappy with the doctors, and I give her the receiving space that is necessary for releasing her discontent that has accumulated over many months. "The kidney–pancreas transplant is not a walk in the park either; during the twenty days in hospital, you have a hard time for six to eight days, and for forty-eight hours you're really ill." The night before the operation, she vomited; this somatic manifestation of distress certainly enabled her to deal with the operation better the next day, and we know that it is important that a patient consciously or unconsciously expresses the anxiety about the surgical operation, because the emotional discharge facilitates the surgeon's work and the healing. She never received any information prior to the transplant; her repeated requests led to an encounter that she describes as Kafkaesque. She was received in an office by two people who asked her the same questions at an interval of a few seconds; this cross-examination had re-immersed her in a particularly frightening atmosphere. The surgeon did not provide her with any information either; she therefore felt extremely anxious in the period leading up to the transplant. She also briefly mentions a delusion under corticotherapy, which is entirely possible but can be remedied medically. "What causes anxiety," she said: "is what happens afterwards; for the first fortnight, they wake you up on the hour, so I didn't rest until I got back home." Like many patients in fact, she mentions the noisy shoes of the night nurses; it goes without saying that at night the patients who cannot get to sleep are acutely aware of ambient noises that tend to be amplified. As will have been understood, Alicia wants to find someone who is compassionate about her painful ordeals, and I understand her very well; but I silently note the emotional tone of the complaint, and I wonder to myself what she is complaining about more specifically?

There was another element to her complaint: she talks to me at great length about her workplace. She is a trained accountant, but she is employed as a cashier in a supermarket. Her medical disability has never been taken into consideration by her boss, a woman whose behaviour, as will be seen later, closely resembles her mother's. She relates in detail the many incidents of workplace harassment to which she has been subjected, especially during the implementation of the thirty-five-hour working week. Tired of battling, she finally wrote to the company president, who asked his executives to respect Alicia's work contract. She left to have the operation without this problem having been resolved, and she was apprehensive about returning. She ends on an ironic note, because her persecutor (her current boss) has herself got into difficulty with one of the male employees who had no respect for the female staff—she thinks because of her cultural background—and who openly expressed his wish to take her place to obtain her benefits and salary.

The problem of returning to work is central for all transplant patients; the scale of their handicap is very rarely taken into consideration by employers before and after the transplant. This is a serious problem that ought to be given careful attention by social workers in organ transplant departments, supported by the public authorities.

Alicia tells me about her diabetes: one woman too many

Alicia begins to tell me her life history and talks continuously for an hour and a half. She was the youngest child in the family in which she grew up; the eldest was a girl who was fourteen years older and whose younger sister died at six days old of the consequences of an operation. The third child was a boy, very impatiently awaited by the father, and two years later she was born. She thinks that her mother does not love her, and her father said on the day she was born that he was disappointed to have a girl. She therefore grew up in a family in which she "had no place," so that in adolescence, at the age of fifteen, she fell ill during the summer. The doctor who was consulted diagnosed diabetes. Both her parents reacted in the same way: "they never accepted my illness," she says: "and life continued in a complete denial of what I was going through." Just as they rejected her illness, they rejected the diet that she was prescribed; this was translated by parapraxes on the mother's part, as she did not understand the medical recommendations. "As a result of the family's diet," Alicia put on more than ten kilos—weight that she never subsequently lost.

Alicia talks to me without showing any emotion, as if she were no longer angry with her parents and as if this were ancient history; there is no tonal variation in her speech. Why? What is happening? Why, having grown up in such a hostile environment, does she show no animosity towards her family? After all, she might be angry.

I know from clinical experience that suppressing the aggressive drives leads, over the long-term, to the development of masochistic behaviour, which may be revealed by this apparently neutral tone, but I need to explore this behaviour more deeply.

A dietician, who was concerned about the observance of the diabetic diet, had given her mother a list of the recommended foods, but this was in vain. Some years later, she had a meeting with a psychologist in a major Paris hospital, to help her to follow her diet better; he asked her questions enigmatically, without telling her the results of his investigation, and her unease only increased. But this silent psychologist helped her beyond her hopes. He advised her to undertake a psychotherapy, writing a letter to refer her to the medical director of the Institute of Psychosomatics in Paris. She kept this letter in her bag for a year, and after a period of reflection she went to the Institute of Psychosomatics, where she met Dr Pierre Marty, who received her warmly in his office; she still remembers this with emotion. This is how random life events enabled me to cross the path that my teacher and friend, now deceased, had taken many years ago when he met Alicia. Following a procedure designed to form an opinion independently and to establish a relationship of trust with the patient without being influenced by the medical file and other letters of recommendation, Pierre Marty began his interview by showing her that he had not opened the letter sent by the psychologist. Alicia was very sensitive to this approach because it had enabled her to express herself, free of the burden of the previous doctors' opinions. Many years later, she still has an extraordinary impression of her meeting with Pierre Marty who, at the end of the interview, recommended her to undertake a psychotherapy that would help her to monitor her diabetes better. This is how she began a psychotherapy with a colleague whom I hold in great esteem and is now retired.

For two and a half years she was treated by her therapist; she remembers with great feeling the first five sessions, to which she travelled in an old car to the Institute of Psychosomatics. She remained silent for forty-five minutes opposite her therapist, completely incapable of opening her mouth. In the fifth session, her therapist—to help her—said to her: "why do you have so much difficulty talking to someone?" and wondered who she was thinking about in her silence. She did not reply immediately, but the question was received, and it was only in the car on the way back that she understood the difficulty she had in communicating with a mother who rejected everything about her and had never accepted her.

This takes us back once again to the hostile family atmosphere that Alicia described in the previous meeting. Suddenly, a thought arose in my mind relating to the circumstances preceding the onset of her diabetes, as I formed the hypothesis of a traumatic event that might have occurred at that time. As if she were listening to my thoughts (at the end of the session she talks to me a great deal about her capacity to perceive other people's thoughts even when they are not communicating with her), Alicia mentions an important event that had occurred in the six months before her diabetes was diagnosed.

She was thirteen years old then, and that year both she and her fifteen-year-old brother had to take the BEPC;[1] she passed her exam but her brother did not. Her brother's failure caused a family drama because everyone was afraid of the father's anger. In the context of this drama, however, no one thought to congratulate Alicia on her success. Once again, a major narcissistic wound was inflicted on her. The whole family spent the rest of the time, and the summer, thinking about her brother's future, because the father's response to his son's failure was to suggest strongly that he continue his studies in the armed forces, more specifically the navy. Alicia was totally forgotten by her family, and many symptoms manifested themselves during that summer. These symptoms had begun a few months earlier: drinking lots of water, up to ten to twelve litres a day, losing weight, and so on, without her mother noticing anything.

Alicia received a double narcissistic wound in the incident described above: a rejection because of her success at school, and a rejection of her femininity that had already been condemned at birth. Subjected to long-term stress in the family, with her narcissism injured, unable to defend herself because of an inhibition of the aggressive drives, we can only assume a de-fusion of the drives causing a progressive disorganisation that is first psychic and then somatic (immune system). In the years that followed, because of the irregular observance of the diabetes treatment, at least two functions were impaired, leading to neuropathy and nephropathy.

Alicia "through the looking glass"

Alicia tells me: "I'm not the same person any more; it's as if my organism had changed after the transplant." Based on her experience, she thought that her body belonged to the doctors: "they wore the white coats; they possessed the truth."

Alicia mentions two different problems: the medical treatment of the diabetes over nearly thirty years, and the recent double transplant. It seems that she is currently noticing some changes: a change in the somatic body image and a change in the psychic image, accompanied by new thoughts about appropriating the body.

She continues by talking about depression (why at this point in our conversation?) She thus explores the problem of changing her body image by an association of ideas. She repeats the problems discussed by patients in the waiting room—problems that give rise to fantasies. Our patients have long discussions together about transplants, about life after the transplant and so on, fantasies that they all have, confusing imagination and reality. She tells me that some patients say that the donor's organs are attacking them and causing dysfunctions. Others think that the depression they are experiencing is caused by the organ from the donor, who was a depressed person.

Alicia records some behavioural changes; she feels more aggressive, and remembers that her psychotherapist had told her at the end of the therapy that she would go through a period in which she would be aggressive towards her mother, which she had not yet allowed herself to do. She leaves her relationship with her mother for a moment to return to the transformations in her body: her legs drag, and she wonders when she will be able to walk normally again; her weight fluctuates a lot, but she lost some when her periods returned. The therapeutic conversations that we have are helping her, she says, to deal with the doctors' criticisms;[2] she feels so dependent on them. She cannot bear to see her abdomen swell; she cannot tolerate her image. "You have to suffer after the transplant, and you're not prepared for that." It seems, though, that the doctors have adopted a "benevolent maternal role" with Alicia.

Her relationship to her body as it undergoes temporary transformations suggests to me that I should give her some explanations to prepare her for accepting the changes. I point out to her that she is experiencing a new birth and that, just as babies are, she is dependent on the medical environment to continue her life, just as she was previously dependent on the parental environment. This first dependence is reactivated because her body will go through the same path, or a similar one; her feeling of powerlessness and bodily transformation generates again in her some remote sensations with which she must gradually become familiar. There is a regression to the relationship of dependency, and as transplant patients are not prepared for it, some may react aggressively; they do not understand what is happening to them, the feeling of powerlessness of the early stages of life returns forcefully, hence the hostility towards the doctors.

The transplants seem to have given Alicia some new strength, and her rediscovered vital tonus is accompanied by aggressive manifestations that I consider highly favourable to the resumption of the psychic maturation process. It goes without saying that the medical staff and doctors do not share my opinion, but I attempt to explain to them our transplant patients' new behaviour by asking them to be tolerant and attentive to such manifestations, which are on the side of life.

At the end of the session, Alicia mentions her thirteen-year-old daughter Emilie's forthcoming confirmation service, and some family relationships that are deteriorating; on Mothering Sunday, her sister and her mother had humiliated her again. She promises herself to tell them everything that she has experienced one day, but this day has not yet arrived.

Alicia's dramatic marriage

Alicia begins by complaining, while laughing, about the doctor who is treating her, because she knows now that he cannot tolerate his patients' aggression; confronted with vertigo spells, he states that they are "psychosomatic". I give heed to this observation, because I think that the doctor must have perceived some unconscious dimensions in the manifestation of this symptom. While protesting against her doctor's excessive attention, Alicia realises that he is making her relive some episodes of maternal dependence. I liken these vertigo spells to distressing episodes in earliest childhood, and ask her to remember her earliest years of life (such as her parents may have reported to her). She tells me that her father revealed to her that her mother never directly took care of the children in their earliest years, which were spent in Africa where he was working. The older children had been educated by the father's former nannies, and some African women looked after her. I have no doubt that her needs were met, but there may have been an emotional lack, as revealed by these symptoms of losing balance and falling. I have noticed in this regard that a great many patients I have treated and interviewed after a recent transplant have presented somatic problems that were unexplained by the doctors. I suggest, as a hypothesis, the reactivation in the post-transplant period of symptoms of distress that were expressed by the body as infants in the preverbal period.

These coenaesthetic problems are being treated by her physiotherapist, who seems to be obtaining some results; highly attentive to the bodily transformations, Alicia seems to perceive something different at present. She thinks, pertinently, that her body has not yet adapted to the transplanted organs. She can no longer tolerate the "maternal" attention and care of her doctor and the nurses. She talks about her weight again; having put on ten kilos is making her suffer, especially because her doctor is criticising her for it,[3] which only exacerbates her guilt. She touches the place in her abdomen where the two transplanted organs are; I then ask her if there is not an analogy with pregnancy, and the sensations that accompany it. She answers negatively and goes on to talk about the probable loss of weight after one or two years; this happened to another patient (in the waiting room). She interprets this weight loss as the body's adaptive reaction to the new condition.

Alicia has returned to work, but her boss is rather disagreeable and cantankerous, just like her mother; he does not value her work and considers her a burden in the department. It must also be emphasised here that employers have not done much to familiarise themselves with our patients' handicaps and do not create a favourable environment for helping them to carry on with their working lives.

She tells me about a forthcoming holiday in the mountains, about which she is slightly apprehensive because she cannot tolerate the altitude. For the first time since our interviews began, she tells me something about her life in the last few years; she met a very elderly priest whom she regards as her adoptive father. This priest had written a book four years earlier that tells her story;[4] he received her into his church, and Alicia "returned to God". The spiritual path was healthy for her after having lived through some dramatic events that I will report very briefly. "Something marvellous happened to me. I found God again and I found someone I could talk to, in whom I could finally have some trust, and who could also be a support for my little girl. And that is a tremendous blessing … I know more than ever that the Lord is there, that Mary is there too."

The spiritual dimension is fundamental to a human being's equilibrium; belief reinforces the capacity to resist adversity. At the end of the session, Alicia tells me her story, which occupies nearly 200 pages of the book. She got married when she was young, to Denis who, when she became pregnant, revealed his deep wish to become a woman, which was what he had always wanted. On her wedding day, Alicia had caught Denis's look of jealousy when admiring her wedding dress; she had felt uneasy about it without being able to attribute a meaning to it at the time. Denis was a transsexual who greatly disrupted Alicia's life; however, she agreed to continue living with Denis, who had become "Denise". Denise's crises and anxieties about her professional life and the acceptance of her new identity plunged her into depressive phases that worsened with the years. After several suicide attempts, Denise finally put an end to her life. It is easier to understand now why Alicia returned to God with a view to saving her life and her psychic equilibrium after such a traumatic marital experience.

Alicia's health returns

As we had arranged, I meet Alicia in the new academic term in September. On arriving at the department, I am very surprised because the doctor says that she is very pleased that I have come. My patient has been in hospital for the last few days, with symptoms that fortunately do not put at risk the double kidney–pancreas transplant.

I go up to the first floor and put on the necessary clothes for entering the sterile room. Alicia is lying outstretched and we greet each other very amicably; I tell her how surprised I am to see her in hospital when I had left her in good health, and ask her what has happened?

Transplants have side-effects, such as skin allergies, and Alicia had been suffering from these for some time. Her dermatologist thought that it was due to the hypocholesterolaemic medication that she was taking. I wonder about the psychic dimension of this symptom; as my patient is very sensitive to this dimension, I keep my thoughts to myself for the moment. I ask her about her life in the last two months. She had taken a holiday in July with her daughter, Emilie, and her adoptive father. They went to the mountains, very high up, and she suffered from the altitude; she feels better when she goes to the Mediterranean coast to stay with a friend of her adoptive father. She has always suffered high up in the mountains. She had gone back to work at the beginning of August and reports that she was feeling much better, as if suddenly she had returned to her state of health before the transplant operations and the dialysis. This state of well-being manifested itself during her return to work and at home, where in a huge upsurge of enthusiasm she wanted to tidy up the attic and her daughter's bedroom.

At her workplace it was the same; her boss had asked her to do a mailshot, a task neglected by her colleagues. She had worked very hard to do it to the great satisfaction of her superiors; she had got deeply involved to show them that her handicap could now be overcome. She tells me in the smallest detail about the efforts she made, her conversations with her superiors, and the satisfaction of having done some work that others could not do.

I consider every aspect of her working and family environment for life events that might have influenced the current functioning. I cannot find anything for the moment, and I continue with my conversation in the hope that "it" will finally be expressed. I ask her to tell me about her dreams recently; after much hesitation, some images appear to her. She feels that she is moving towards a woman who is caressing her; some other people are present. The many associations lead to the mother–daughter relationship in the early months and years of life, and to the baby's demands to be caressed; as we know clinically and medically (Spitz, 1965), the baby often expresses his emotional distress through skin allergies (the quantum of excitation being localised in the epidermis). This desire to rediscover maternal affection (in a psychic homosexual way that disturbed the patient when she recounted her dream) that she lacked re-emerges in consequence of the psychosomatic unity having been restored by the double transplant.

She has experienced some physical changes in the past two months, with a very strong increase in libido. First there was the return of her periods, then the desire to have loving relations again—a desire that is currently difficult to live out because she has not yet recovered from her past experiences. I tell her that she is still a young woman, and that she must allow herself to live out freely the return of life inside her; I also tell her that the libido is the sign of the return of life.

Throughout the session, she complains about the relations with one of the doctors in the department who has, in some way, made her relive her mother's persecutions; I must add here, because I have not explained it earlier, that the masochistic component of her personality enabled her to get through all the ordeals in her life, from the discovery of her diabetes to the present day.

A catheter was inserted into her to drain the amylase from the pancreas; she hates catheters and strongly resisted the doctor by refusing to take the tranquilliser he had prescribed following the criticisms she had made. She experienced the doctor's prescription as a punishment; Alicia constantly repeats with her doctors her early relations with her mother. She is suffering from a skin allergy and pancreatitis. She talks at great length about this suffering, which very obviously has a somatic origin and is aggravated by all the work of moving cardboard boxes around at home. She agrees with this; her adoptive father had drawn her attention to the excessive fatigue caused by this activity. She strongly emphasises the doctors' ignorance about patients' sexual lives and their fears of talking about it. I repeat to her that I notice a resumption of Eros activity that I interpret as a very positive sign of better bodily functioning, and therefore of the transplanted organs.

I give a very positive prognosis concerning the progress of this patient, who draws our attention to the resumption of the life drives caused by a return of bodily homeostasis. To eliminate any biological danger that might influence the psychic functioning, I encourage her doctor to continue the investigations. It is important to know that pancreas transplants are more problematic (there are approximately six pancreas transplants a year) than other types of transplant.

I meet Alicia again because she is still hospitalised on the first floor of our department. I had obtained some information from the nurses, who had reassured me that her state of health was gradually improving. When I go back into her room, she is sitting in her armchair smiling, while taking her breakfast. Our whole conversation relates to the doctor–patient relationship; she first talks to me at length about her somatic symptoms, namely pancreatitis. She had never really been informed about the risks of the pancreas transplant; no doctor or surgeon ever told her what somatic incidents she would be confronted with in the first year after the surgery.

She explains that she agreed to the transplant because she regards herself as a young woman and she deeply wants to be present for a long time for her daughter, who is now thirteen years old. But after nine months since the transplant, she is dealing with the first incidents; it is her discussions with patients in the waiting room that have informed her about what can happen after such a transplant. She worries a lot about the consequences of her pancreatitis, because she must insert the catheter herself to reduce the inflammation of the pancreas, which makes it possible to empty her bladder and therefore to reduce the risk of inflammation. Now she must repeat this operation at least six times a day, which presents her with a great many problems that worry her deeply, and make her relive the period of the diabetes in which she was herself administering six injections daily. What then is the benefit of the transplant if there is an obligation that occurs every day? She must take all the materials with her in her bag and perform this operation every time she goes to the toilet.

During our conversation, two nurses come to take her blood pressure and the result reveals hypotension. We then talk about her breakfast and what she is eating, but again Alicia worries about her weight because she has put on four more kilos—fourteen kilos in total since the transplant. She is worried about her waistline because she does not want to look like her mother, with whom she has affectionate and hostile relations. She wants to go on a diet, but her hypotension and her hypoglycaemia are not really being taken into consideration by the doctor, who thinks that her level of 0.70g is excellent.

She then tells me that the doctors seem to overlook the whole psychological state of the diabetic patient, who can be weakened somatically when moving from a level of 4g to a level of 0.90g. The doctor takes account of neither the bodily effect caused by the reduced level nor its psychological repercussions.[5] Alicia is considered by her doctor to be a grumpy and aggressive patient, who is behaving capriciously in some way. When she shows her disagreement, he walks away from her or turns his back on her when he is in the room.

For her future treatment, the doctor recommends intravenous drips, and Alicia says once again that he never asks himself any questions about the duration of the drip or the suffering this may cause and the various somatic risks, namely that: "the vein may burst and that it will be necessary to inject again somewhere else, often in the hand, which is especially painful … A doctor never wonders about his patients' capacities to deal with the prescriptions he makes," she emphasises. I readily acknowledge that all these criticisms may be difficult for the doctors to hear, but my colleagues must understand that the return of aggressive manifestations and human resistance in patients must be interpreted as a return of life that is due to all their care.

It is important that the aggressive drives can be openly expressed, because they are a means of discharging the intrapsychic tensions; where impulses are suppressed, there is a danger they will return against the patient and aggravate the somatisation. I know how difficult it is for the medical staff and doctors to deal with such manifestations.

We part on an optimistic note, because Alicia is thinking about spending the weekend with her family and returning to work. She wishes deeply to be at her daughter's side to support her at school this year. She is feeling much better, and I strongly recommend her to undertake a supportive psychotherapy.[6]

Two years after the transplant, Alicia's quality of life has improved considerably, because the double transplant has enabled the body to restore a somatic equilibrium without this actually amounting to a return to the previous equilibrium. In the psychic domain, the re-fusion of the drives, a sign of life, has gradually enabled her to experience loving feelings (return of libido), and above all to be able to learn about saying "no"—finally to express her aggressive drives without feeling guilty; her return to professional activity is nearly satisfactory, with the spiritual dimension giving her stability and serenity.

It should be understood that after a long illness caused by an organ deficiency, two transplant operations, and many other ordeals, I find that Alicia now has a satisfactory quality of life, and this viewpoint is shared.

CHAPTER SEVEN

The heart problems of a "famous patient"

I began to read the works of Sigmund Freud when I was fifteen years old; my philosophy teacher had strongly recommended him to us, and so the *Introductory Lectures* became my companion for many years. I still have this book in my library now many years later and, in 1973, I became a practising psychoanalyst, then a few years later a psychosomatician psychoanalyst. In this distant period of my adolescence, I experienced a trauma following my doctor's announcement that my eye problems were going to result in blindness and that I was not going to be able to study medicine. Healing was my vocation, and I refused to contemplate the prospect of living in darkness for the rest of my life. However, for three months I had to live in a totally darkened room to protect my eyes. I understand better now the depression that gradually formed in me following the affliction of the body; the doctors of this period knew nothing about psychoanalysis or psychotherapies, because for them my depression belonged to psychiatry. My life was very difficult for three years, and my only companion was Sigmund Freud; my maternal grandfather, whom I very much loved, was the same age and I naturally developed a strong emotional transference to the father of psychoanalysis—I conversed with him every time I read his work. Since that time, I have had a particular relationship with that man, who is both a scientific reference point and the person who helped me when I was painstakingly advancing in the uncertain realm of my unconscious to move towards the light.

At a study day in 2010, at the Société de psychosomatique intégrative (which I founded with my colleagues trained in this discipline at the Faculty of Medicine), I presented a paper on Sigmund Freud's heart problems because it seemed to me, having scanned through the scientific literature, that few people had wondered about the nature of these problems or, at the very least, that their importance had been underestimated. Also, as my cardiologist colleague, Professor Daniel Thomas, was taking part in the teaching for the university diploma in integrative psychosomatics, I thought I would send him all my observations on the "patient's file" to obtain his commentaries.

That is the story of the final case in this book, and I will quote the text of my paper:

> My interest in Sigmund Freud's somatic problems[1] dates back to 1999 in connection with cancer patients, when I began to turn my attention to the somatic history of his known problems (cardiac and jaw cancer). The psychoanalytic journals that I was reading did not seem to be concerned with the cardiac problems experienced by the father of psychoanalysis. At that time I was collecting data from somatic patients with a view to writing a book and I was re-reading the works of Didier Anzieu and Max Schur, Freud's doctor. These two authors led me to take a closer interest in Freud's "illnesses".

The symptoms described by Freud

I am initially going to draw up a description of the problems based on my notes, then I will try to elaborate the case. In the chapter "Freud's cardiac episode: the battle against nicotine addiction", Max Schur (1972) refers to the extremely stressful situations that Freud managed to overcome. Freud's correspondence with Fliess, and his self-analysis between 1892 and 1902, is important for understanding Freud's problems. In this correspondence, Freud made frequent reference to many physical symptoms: headaches, which Freud called "migraine attacks" (Schur, 1972, p. 40), a nasal problem that may have been caused by a chronic sinus infection, and some indeterminate gastrointestinal symptoms. The cardiac symptoms are by far the most important. Freud first refers to his heart problems in a letter of 18 October 1893, which tells us that the question had already been addressed with Fliess. From the outset, Fliess attributes this symptom mainly to tobacco, because he thought that nicotine considerably aggravated these problems. This marked the beginning of an endless series of attempts by Freud to give up tobacco. Freud promises not to smoke, but he uses the German word *peinlich*, which means both *painfully* and *painstakingly*; in the same letter, he announces to Fliess an imminent aggravation of his heart condition. He also writes that he is feeling better despite the fact that he is smoking a lot. The subject of death begins to appear in his letters: "I am not obeying your order not to smoke; do you really consider it a remarkable boon to live a great many years in misery?" (Masson, 1985, p. 61). The thoughts of death that preoccupied him suddenly find an echo in the announcement, on 7 February 1894, of the death of a famous surgeon, a close friend of Brahms, Théodore Billroth; Freud admired him greatly for his diverse talents.

In another letter, on 19 April 1894, Freud mentions his difficulties in tolerating the abstinence from smoking and, above all, his "cardiac misery" being worse than before he had given up cigars:

> Less obvious, perhaps, is the state of my health in other respects. Soon after the withdrawal, there were some tolerable days ... then suddenly there came a severe cardiac misery, greater than I ever had while smoking. The most violent arrhythmia, constant tension, pressure, burning in the heart region; shooting pains down my left arm; some dyspnea, all of it essentially in attacks extending continuously over two-thirds of the day; the dyspnea is so moderate that one suspects something organic; and with it a feeling of depression, which took the form of visions of death and departure in place of the usual frenzy of activity. The organic discomforts have lessened during the past two days; the lypemanic [hypomanic] mood persists, having the courtesy, though, to let up suddenly (as it did last night and at noon today) and leave behind a human being who looks forward with confidence again to a long life and undiminished pleasure in resuming the battle. (Masson, 1985, p. 67)

Freud wonders how, as: "a medical man who spends every hour of the day struggling to gain an understanding of the neuroses," he can tell if he himself is experiencing a depression with a justifiable cause, or a hypochondriac depression.

Faced with symptoms of this kind, a psychosomatician would want first to explore the hypothesis of a real organic problem, then would wonder about the depressive syndrome following the patient's excessively rapid withdrawal from tobacco. The hypochondriac hypothesis would be quickly eliminated because, until the age of thirty-eight, the patient had never exhibited the slightest behaviour of this kind when functional problems occurred. In fact, Freud is lucid enough to realise that the neuropathological explanation must be set aside for the time being.

He turns to Breuer, telling him that, in his opinion, the cardiac problems were due not to a nicotine poisoning but more probably to a chronic myocarditis, "which does not tolerate smoking" (Masson, 1985, p. 67). According to his hypothesis, the cardiac arrhythmia dates back to 1889 and is the consequence of an episode of influenza.

Schur's description of the cardiac problems suggests to him that these were attacks of paroxysmal tachycardia, probably with auricular fibrillation, along with signs of coronary deficiency such as anginal pains and dyspnoea.

In relation to his attacks, Freud talks about a depression accompanied by a vision of death and leave-taking. Under strong emotional pressure, Freud gives a very strange description of his symptoms; Max Schur only quotes the German text, because the English translation seems to be wrong. He thinks that the sentences were written in a time of psychic stress and reveal a situation that could be described as "traumatic," in Freud's own terminology (Schur, 1972, p. 45).

He refers to the psychic stress that Freud was caused by three attacks that persisted for part of the day, and that continued in the days that followed. Schur supposes that when Freud refers to his hypomanic [sic] state, he is using the mechanism of denial; denial of his depression. Freud wants to rediscover the pleasure of smoking—*Rauchlust*—and he makes a slip of the pen: *rauflust*, meaning "combative spirit", which expresses Freud's wish to rediscover the pleasure of smoking and not as Schur says "to *fight* for his right to smoke" (1972, p. 46) (Schur's analysis refers to a parapraxis on Freud's part, whereas I think it is only a slip of the pen).

The end of Freud's letter to Fliess reveals the behaviour that he later adopts in his battle against cancer. As Schur comments: "The words 'from every point of view' clearly meant: 'If my worry is unfounded, why let my wife participate in it? If I really am suffering from a fatal illness, why cause her anguish years ahead of time?'" (Schur, 1972, p. 47, footnote 16; see also letter to Eitingon of 1 April 1925, p. 382). Freud does not want to worry his family and prefers to keep his sufferings to himself.

On 6 May 1894, his thirty-eighth birthday, Freud sets aside the hypothesis that the nicotine is causing his heart problems and puts forward instead one of rheumatismal myocarditis, "something one never really gets rid of" (Masson, 1985, p. 70). Freud suggested this having encountered many phenomena of the same kind in some of his patients.

It should be remembered that, at this time, Freud is dealing with illness, abstinence, and isolation, and that he is fighting alone in attempting to discover the origins of neurosis. He is just finishing his *Studies on Hysteria*.

I must emphasise here a very important point in Freud's behaviour, which concerns the relationship between the patient and the doctor. Freud was not convinced that Breuer was telling him the truth; he was afraid that Fliess was also concealing it from him. Freud pleads with Fliess to be honest. Schur states in this regard:

> We frequently hear assertions from patients that they can accept with full dignity the knowledge of serious and even fatal illness, but find that they actually do not wish to know the truth, and may even break down under its impact. Freud, however, meant what he said, as he was subsequently to prove. (Schur, 1972, pp. 46–47)

The letter of 19 April sheds light on the difficult problem of the nicotine dependency that was to trouble Freud throughout his life. In another letter, in May 1894, Freud questions Breuer's diagnosis; he mentions the possibility of myocarditis. However, he indicates that there is no cardiac dilatation but that the heart murmurs (an important sign of organic lesion), arrhythmia, and so on are persisting despite the abstinence. Freud complains of a bad mood, fatigue, an incapacity to work, and mild dyspnoea. He takes 1g of digitalin every other day; he thinks that the digitalin has had an effect on the cardiac arrhythmia.

In the letter of 6 May 1894, on his thirty-eighth birthday, Freud indicates that he has not yet been able to finish the draft on the neuroses; he has not had more than half a day free of symptoms and his mood and his capacity to work have never been so low.

The illness, the tobacco abstinence, the isolation, and the solitary struggle he began by endeavouring to discover the origins of neurosis and, therefore, to shed light on the functional mechanisms of the human mind seem to be weighing heavily on his equilibrium and his mood. Can this be seen as the price paid by Freud for discovering what was to be psychoanalysis? This is the question I ask myself, as is suggested by the letter of 21 May 1894: "I am pretty much alone here in the elucidation of the neuroses. They look upon me as pretty much of a monomaniac, while I have the distinct feeling that I have touched upon one of the great secrets of nature" (Masson, 1985, p. 74). It is during this period that he completes the *Studies on Hysteria*.

On 22 June 1894, Freud writes:

> I have not smoked for seven weeks, since the day of your prohibition. At first ... cardiac symptoms accompanied by mild depression, as well as the horrible misery of abstinence. The latter wore off after approximately three weeks, the former abated after about five weeks, but it left me completely incapable of working, a beaten man. After seven weeks, despite my promise to you, I began smoking again. (Masson, 1985, p. 84)

Freud returns to smoking around three cigars a day and states that he feels better than before:

> Some arrhythmia always seems to be present, but intensification to a delirium cordis with oppression occurs only in attacks, now lasting less than an hour and setting in almost regularly after lunch. The moderate dyspnea while climbing steps is gone; the left arm has been free of pain for weeks; the chest wall is still quite tender; stabbing pains, the feeling of oppression, burning sensations have not let up for a day. Objective evidence can apparently not be found, but then I really do not know. Sleep and all other functions are entirely undisturbed; I am in good control of my moods; on the other hand, I feel aged, sluggish, not healthy. Digitalis has helped me tremendously ... What tortures me is the uncertainty about what to make of the story. It would embarrass me to suggest a hypochondriacal evaluation, but I have no criteria by which to decide this. (Masson, 1985, p. 84)

On 14 July 1894, he writes:

> Since your letter of Thursday a fortnight ago, abstinence, which lasted eight days; on the following Thursday, in an indescribably bleak moment, one cigar; then again eight days abstinence; the following Thursday one more, since then peace. In brief, a pattern has established itself—one cigar a week. (Masson, 1985, p. 87)

From July 1894, it seems that the crisis had come to an end, and although Freud suffered from problems during 1895 his mood was optimistic. On 23 August 1894, he refers to the improvement in his heart symptoms. Two years before the death of his father, he visits his parents. who were staying in Ischl.

Dr Max Schur's summary diagnosis

Schur naturally asks himself many questions about how to establish a diagnosis approximately 75 years after the events. He summarises the case as follows:

1. Freud notices an arrhythmia following a feverish illness, probably influenza contracted in 1889. In April 1894, at the time of his symptoms, he remembers this problem.
2. In spring 1894, the heart problems worsen, as detailed in letters dated 19 and 25 April, 6 May, and 22 June 1894. For several weeks, Freud has daily attacks, severe arrhythmias and tachycardia with anginal pain, and a mild dyspnoea that seriously restricts his physical activity. His doctor thinks that, at the time of the most severe attacks, the patient is suffering from paroxysmal tachycardia, probably accompanied by auricular fibrillation.
3. The three doctors—Freud himself, Breuer, and Fliess—considered two possibilities: chronic myocarditis and nicotine poisoning. Breuer favoured the first hypothesis and Fliess the second; Freud oscillated between the two hypotheses.
4. Schur thinks that other diagnoses are possible: he considers chronic myocarditis to be too vague—this is due to the lack of clinical investigation methods that are known today. He thinks that, during the spring of 1894, Freud must have suffered a *coronary thrombosis*.

Freud referred to "painful nodules" (Schur, 1972, p. 57) in his muscles, which does not allow us to infer though that he was suffering from acute articular rheumatism with cardiac complications. His subsequent heart condition in no way justifies such a conclusion. He puts forward another possibility, which is an acute infectious myocarditis of indeterminate origin.

5. The syndrome of paroxysmal tachycardia with or without auricular fibrillation is well-known. It can appear without any noticeable trace of organic lesion. The pseudo-anginal pain and dyspnoea can be explained by the coronary deficiency that may have been caused by the more persistent attacks. Acute anxiety can sometimes trigger attacks that are then considered as anxiety manifestations.

6. In patients prone to vasovagal reflex, a wide range of sensory stimuli and emotional stress can trigger many circulatory problems. In patients suffering from chest angina, this same reflex can cause an attack of angina (*angor pectoris*). Other problems encountered are nauseous reactions, vomiting, diarrhoea, or signs of colonic spasms or colic irritability with mucomembranous enterocolitis. Freud experienced problems of this kind several times in his life. Freud's fainting fits (he is known to have had four or five) always occurred in situations of intense stress. The colitis attacks and the short periods of frequent extrasystoles were caused by excessive tobacco and alleviated by a small dose of belladonna.

7. Schur rules out the hypothesis of a particular hypersensitivity to nicotine, because then the acute attacks would have coincided more or less regularly with the return to smoking cigars with severe cardiovascular reactions that would have recurred periodically throughout his life, because Freud always remained a heavy smoker; *these attacks did not recur*. Freud lived for another forty-five years and he never had another attack of paroxysmal tachycardia with auricular fibrillation.

8. Jones puts forward a diagnosis of severe psychoneurosis with a peak phase that he locates in the latter half of the 1890s and suggests that Freud "would later doubtless have classified it as an anxiety hysteria" (1972, p. 335). Schur raises some questions: how does Jones explain the psychoneurotic nature of all these problems? Does he think there was an organic neurosis, a somatisation of conflicts and/or anxiety, or something that we would now call a "psychosomatic"

condition? Or does he believe that it was merely a hypochondriac development from some occasional extrasystoles? During his lifetime, Freud only expressed anxieties about death twice in all his correspondence: in the letters of 19 April 1894 and 16 April 1896, concerning the sculptor Tilgner's death from a heart attack. Freud's mood was very depressive when his heart problems extended to a paroxysm; for Schur: "if a person expresses pessimistic views, is depressed and even afraid of death during a period of severe cardiovascular distress, this in no way proves that these symptoms represent the somatization of an unconscious conflict or of excessive, uncontrolled anxiety" (1972, p. 60).

9. Schur suggests the hypothesis of an organic lesion with temporary failures of the left ventricle. To support this hypothesis, he returns to the symptoms mentioned by Freud, which he thinks are angina attacks; namely, severe pains in the left arm and a feeling of suffocation. The tachycardia and arrhythmia attacks are common phenomena in this illness, he states. During this period, Freud showed signs of a slight left ventricular failure, such as shortness of breath or what he later described as "motoric insufficiency" (1972, p. 61). He emphasises that Freud reacted positively to repeated and irregular doses of digitalin for over a year. He points out that a coronary thrombosis can occur at a relatively young age (Freud was thirty-eight in 1894) and he thinks that it is not possible for someone who has angina symptoms for decades to maintain a normal cardiac functioning.

In conclusion, Schur puts forward the following hypotheses based on the various observations:

> *To sum up*: We have no valid reason for subscribing to Jones's theory that "all these troubles were … special aspects of his psychoneurosis" (Vol. 1, p. 311). I am inclined to the opinion that between late 1893 and 1896 Freud suffered from attacks of paroxysmal tachycardia, with anginal pain and signs of left ventricular failure; that these attacks reached their peak during April, 1894, at which point he suffered an organic myocardial lesion, most likely a coronary thrombosis in a small artery, or perhaps a postinfectious myocarditis, with temporarily increased nicotine sensitivity. (Schur, 1972, p. 62)

Concerning nicotine and tobacco, there is a letter by Sigmund Freud of 12 February 1929:

> I began smoking at the age of 24, first cigarettes but soon exclusively cigars, and am still smoking now (at 72½), and very reluctant to restrict myself in this pleasure. Between the ages of 30 and 40 I had to give up smoking for a year and a half because of heart trouble which may have been [due to] the effect of nicotine, but was probably a sequel to influenza. Since then I have been faithful to my habit or vice, and believe that I owe to the cigar a great intensification of my capacity to work and a facilitation of my self-control. My model in this was my father, who was a heavy smoker and remained one till his 81st year. (Schur, 1972, p. 62)

9.3 Prof Daniel Thomas's assessment[2]

I passed the above notes to my cardiologist colleague at La Pitié-Salpêtrière (Institut de cardiologie) to obtain his opinion about a probable diagnosis that he might make based on contemporary medical knowledge.

Here are the observations that I am able to make based on the information you have provided to me:

1. Given the age at which the heart problems emerged (before the age of 40 years), it might initially be thought that this is not a coronary pathology. But his description of the symptoms as "pressure … burning pains down the left arm … chest pain irradiating into the left arm" (Schur, 1972, pp. 43–44), the circumstances (he does not mention any connection with effort), and the tobacco addiction does not rule out coronary spasms, manifestations of which usually occur at rest and are seen almost exclusively in smokers. Even at the end of the nineteenth century, Huchard was already describing in his treaty of medicine "tobacco angina", which became a reality of modern cardiology when the coronary spasm and its demonstration at the time of the coronarography was put on show in the 1980s. I even remember a presentation by a team from Boucicaut hospital to the Société Française de Cardiologie that had conducted a coronarography with slides taken before and then after a cigarette

had been smoked, which clearly showed the reduction in size of the coronary arteries ...

But it should also be noted that tachycardia attacks can lead to functional angina since he reports a correlation with painful rhythmic symptoms.

The hypothesis of an acute coronary thrombosis at such an early age is also possible in a smoker. However, it seems highly improbable, even if this possibility is not totally excluded, that he would have reached such an advanced age without any further coronary problem.

Therefore, if there is any underlying coronary pathology, it is a coronary spasm.

NB: Freud was perspicacious enough to mention the role played by tobacco himself later in this letter of 12 February 1929 that is quoted at the end of your text.

2. The heart rhythm problems are less likely to be directly connected with his tobacco addiction, even if they might be fostered by it given that they seem to be alleviated when he temporarily stopped smoking. However, at this age, rhythm problems, which do not seem to have recurred subsequently (?), may correspond to the benign supraventricular tachycardias of Bouveret's disease, which occur more readily in young subjects and usually those with a healthy heart, but can be disturbing, given the increased heart rate and sometimes accompanying sensations of thoracic pains.

An auricular fibrillation is less probable because although he uses the term "arrythmias", he does not directly refer to the irregularity of the heart rate in describing the symptoms. Digitalin, which was then the only available remedy for arrhythmia, seems to have had an effect ... but it has had no specific effect on "a type" of rhythm problem, so this is not highly informative.

It is not impossible that a psychoneurosis might have been having an impact on these functional phenomena, in particular rhythmic ones, by means of the neurovegetative system. The autonomic nervous system is known to be one of three elements that intervene in triggering arrhythmias: this is the famous arrhythmogenic "triangle" with: the "substrate" (the ailing cardiac muscle or the fibrosis formed in the muscle), the "trigger" (the extrasystoles that are in fact present to a greater or lesser degree in most individuals without necessarily having any consequences) and the "regulating factors", the most dominant being the autonomic nervous system.

3. Finally, the term "chronic myocarditis" that is mentioned covered at that time the ignorance of unlabelled pathologies and should not be taken into account, in my view, although it is mentioned by the exegetes who have studied how to interpret the great man's heart pains.

A link between the influenza infection in 1889 and the infectious episode that occurred in 1894 is therefore not very plausible.

To conclude, we can of course only establish an enlightened "probability" in retrospect. It is easy enough to make mistakes in the diagnostic approach even in real time … the archaeological reading of past pathologies therefore seems to me to be a much more difficult exercise in which we must demonstrate great restraint (Prof Daniel Thomas, personal communication).

Daniel Thomas's probable diagnosis attests the physical origin of Freud's heart symptoms during these few years in which he worked out the first scientific corpus of psychoanalysis, combined with his personal neurotic problems, as Jones supposed. Here it is a matter of the psychic subjective dimension of a bodily problem that was well analysed and described in fact by Freud, who was initially a doctor, himself. This is not of course a hypochondriac problem; as in every somatic problem, and in this particular case, it is accompanied by a depressive syndrome connected with tobacco privation, which has psychic effects that must never be underestimated. Equally, the high quantum of excitations connected with Freud's considerable intellectual efforts to achieve the discovery of psychoanalysis should be reintroduced into the explanation of these organic problems. Freud was overwhelmed by the excitations connected with his investigations; Schur's statements about the psychosomatic dimension or organic neurosis are no longer up-to-date; this is the previous approach to psychosomatic illness that was challenged by the Paris School and its founder, Pierre Marty.

CHAPTER EIGHT

Conclusion

Being on the side of life and supporting the life drives is the psychosomatician's fundamental mission.
As can be seen with some of the patients whose clinical examination and/or therapeutic progression I have outlined, the first stage is to rebuild the unity of psychosomatic life. In this stage, because of the psychic regression caused by the illness, the psychosomatician psychotherapist adopts an empathic and warm standpoint towards his patient, and, in parallel with the essential medical treatments, he gradually strengthens the patient's ego so that this agency can recathect the various domains of life. In this stage, the psychosomatician adopts a maternal attitude of narcissistic repair to patients; in most cases, this is not the usual psychoanalytic transference relationship but an attachment relationship as defined by Bowlby. For many of our patients the transference neurosis has never been established, and we must gradually build and rebuild their life history, which ensures the continuity of functioning and the stability of the psychic apparatus.

Once the psychosomatic unity has been restored, the psychic functioning often resumes in a remarkable way, according to the patient's previous mental structuring (in terms of fixation-regression points); in many cases, the interrupted oedipal problematic resumes for various reasons and we move into the second stage that is much more classical and familiar to psychoanalysts.

In the economic dimension of psychic functioning, the patient's libido, mobilised by the somatic problems, is freed of this rescuing cathexis, and the patient regains more and more vital energy as the libido returns; in the psychodynamic dimension, the conflicts reappear, thanks to the restored density of the preconscious, and capacities to move back and forth between the present and the past. It involves long and detailed but absolutely vital work to build or rebuild mental representations; as Marty and Bion have strongly recommended, this can only be done by lending patients what is called "the apparatus for dealing with thoughts".

Once this therapeutic work has been done and the objective of stabilisation and homoeostasis of the psychosomatic unity is achieved, we can provisionally put an end to the treatment, while telling the patient that we are available to him at any time to support him or to continue the work done previously. It is important that our patients regain some autonomy and stability; we must also trust in the "mysterious" processes of the cellular life that restores the individual homeostasis. After all, we cannot keep our patients "eternally" in psychotherapy.

The progression of Chloé's psychotherapy (Chapter Two), and the neuropsychoanalysis movement created by Mark Solms in the 1990s, shed light on a dimension so far overlooked by psychoanalysts and psychotherapists, namely that the psychic work is strongly supported by, and interconnected with, the neuronal networks. It takes on average nine to eighteen months to strengthen, structure, restructure, or create neuronal networks in a psychosomatic psychotherapeutic relationship. The belief that psychotherapeutic work is exclusively verbal in being limited to the psychic domain has ended; our work operates with the aid of the cerebral plasticity that continues until the end of life itself. This is the extraordinary discovery of the last twenty years that must be taken into consideration when we become involved in sensitive therapeutic work. I remember that Freud talked about construction in analysis; was he not implicitly referring to the CNS structures that underlie the psychic apparatus?

All the cortices are brought into play in the therapeutic relationship: the hippocampus and all the memory systems, the limbic system, all the emotional circuits, the associative cortices, sensorimotor cortices, and so on. No one can create an abstraction from the existence of the neuronal networks and their synaptic restructuring. It would be interesting to do some psychoanalytic research on the nature of so-called "mutative" interpretations and the development of neuronal structures. I suggest introducing knowledge of the neurosciences for training future generations of psychoanalysts.

The practice of psychosomatics is difficult; as in the case of *The Little Prince* (Chapter Three), we are dealing with very high-risk patients. It is often at a very late stage that we are consulted, and we can only accompany a deadly movement or slow its advance, but no one can counteract death. I met this patient fifteen years too late; I did everything I could to support him and to slow down a complex process in which the death drive was manifesting itself more and more. Just like doctors, the psychosomatician—unlike his psychoanalyst colleagues—must integrate into his practice the possibility that he will see his patients disappear.

As concerns medicine, I wish for a profound change in the medical training programme, such that the authorities in medical faculties will introduce knowledge of the functioning of the psychic apparatus in relation to all the somatic systems. This is a long way off for the time being; unlike the approaches taken in North America and Germany, which adopted psychosomatic medicine over sixty years ago now, France still adheres to the first paradigm of medicine—the paradigm of man as a machine, radically separating the psychic apparatus from the body.

We are dealing with a high-tech medicine that leaves little or no room for human subjects and leads to all the familiar problems: difficulties in doctor–patient relations, announcements of severe diagnoses, understanding patients' behaviour in therapeutic observance, support given to families, and so on. It is time to introduce the patient alongside the illness and to adopt the second paradigm of medicine that allows space for the subject. We can understand how, because of the emphasis on the techno-biological dimension, alternative medicines have developed to compensate for the relational deficit with patients; in this way, many patients have turned away from the contemporary medical movement.

This is what Stefan Zweig wrote in relation to Sigmund Freud in 1932 in his book *Mental Healers*:

> In the hospitals … the sick are put into separate departments, just as in a business undertaking the various sections are differentiated one from another. The doctors, too, are highly specialized; they go from bed to bed examining the diseased organ and hardly ever find time to look into the eyes of the human being whose suffering

> needs relief ... a large-scale industry arises, in the running of which there is never a moment's leisure for personal contact between physician and patient, and wherein there is no longer a trace of magnetic rapport between the soul of the healer and the soul of the healed. (1933, pp. xv–xvi)

Since the end of the twentieth century, hospital professors and doctors have become aware of the limitations of technologised medicine. They have introduced information and, above all, the therapeutic education of patients in some departments. This involves a transmission of medical knowledge and skill as part of a multidisciplinary approach; the main objective is to improve the quality of the care provided, taking into consideration all the dimensions of human beings: biological, psychological, sociocultural, and spiritual. These steps are to be strongly encouraged because they are complementary to integrative psychosomatics. However, we must insist on the requirement of training in psychoanalysis of trainers who, for the time being, know nothing about the functioning of the psychic apparatus of the patients they want to help. We must insist on the knowledge and recognition of the psychic apparatus, since the results anticipated by doctors are exclusively based on a cognitive approach (information about knowledge and skills) and an improbable change in patients' behaviours. Some new stages have to be gone through before we can provide truly effective help to our patients; we cannot improvise being a psychotherapist.

It is now nineteen years ago that I undertook a long journey that was recommended to me by Pierre Marty when I was president of IPSO (Institute of Psychosomatics); he deeply wished for psychosomaticians to be appointed in hospitals to sensitise our medical colleagues to psychosomatics. I think I have fulfilled this mission, to the extent that I have been able to develop an integrative psychosomatics practice that is open to all the departments at La Pitié-Salpêtrière, and to establish the university diploma in integrative psychosomatics with the help of two colleagues, Professors Jean-François Allilaire and Marc-Olivier Bitker. It is now for the professionals, doctors, and psychotherapists who have obtained this diploma to pursue this mission, each in their specific professional environment.

I wish with all my heart that the times to come will explore more deeply, as Stefan Zweig said: "the close relationship which exists between body and mind, a relationship which in the future may be made clearer to us and more understandable" (ibid., pp. xxi).

NOTES

Foreword

1. Pierre Marty died in June 1993. He founded the Paris School of Psychosomatics in the early 1960s, and in 1978 he founded the Institute of Psychosomatics (IPSO) at the Poterne des Peupliers hospital (Paris 75013). I worked with him from 1984, and I was president of the IPSO from 1989 to 1992.
2. When Freud declared his support for non-medic psychoanalysts, this was Reich's reply to him. I would like to thank my former student and colleague Stéphane Flamant for drawing my attention to this text.
3. Lawrence Schlesinger Kubie (1896–1973) was an American neurologist and psychotherapist known in particular for his works on hypnosis (1954, 1961).
4. Leopold Szondi (1893–1986) was a Hungarian doctor and psychopathologist and the founder of "fate analysis". His investigations—influenced by Freud and Binswanger—concerned heredity and genetic theories.
5. Mustapha Ziwar (1907–1990), an Egyptian psychosomatician, was one of the pioneers of psychosomatic medicine in France and the founder of the psychoanalytic movement in the Arab world. In 1950, he established the first psychology department in the Arab countries at Ain Shams University in Cairo; he taught Safouan, who translated

Freud's *Interpretation of Dreams* into Arabic and introduced Jacques Lacan's thought into the Arab-Muslim world.
6. I recommend reading the excellent sixth issue (published in 1994) of the *Revue Française de Psychosomatique*, which is devoted to Pierre Marty following his death in June 1993. At this time, I was still a member of this journal's scientific committee.
7. Marty, P., Herzberg, R., Stora, J. B. (1987). Organisation psychosomatique et risque de cancer (psychosomatic organisation and cancer risk), research in December 1987, unpublished manuscript.

Marty, P., Stora, J. B. (1988). La Classification psychosomatique Marty/Ipso, méthode d'aide au diagnostic des organisations psychosomatiques et des maladies somatiques (the Marty/IPSO psychosomatic classification, a diagnostic tool for psychosomatic organisations and somatic illnesses). *Médecine et Hygiène*. Also published in 1989, La clasificacion psicosomatica MARTY/IPSO: metodo diagnostico de las organizaciones psicosomaticas y enfermedades somaticas, *Psicoterapia Analitica*, Vol. 1, n° 1, pp. 19–31.

Stora, J. B., Marty, P., Gautier, J. -M. (1989). Sémiologie psychosomatique (psychosomatic semiology). *C.R n° 331: Groupe HEC*, 1989.

Marty, P., Stora, J. B. (1989), *Psychosomatiques*, ed. Beyrouth, in Arabic. 175 p.

Introduction

1. At the psychoanalytic institute of the Paris Psychoanalytical Society.
2. Sándor Ferenczi developed an active technique that was strongly criticised by Freud and the psychoanalytic community of the time. Ferenczi had many patients suffering from somatic illnesses, to whom the classical psychoanalytic technique was not applicable, which has been the source of many misunderstandings.
3. Dr Pauline W. Chen, "Putting Barriers between doctor and patient"— discussion on the Well Blog, published October 21, 2010.
4. As co-director of the university diploma in Integrative Psychosomatics, I organise an annual symposium on a field of medicine in relation to psychosomatics with the Société de Psychosomatique Intégrative and the professors in charge of the hospital's medical departments.
5. cf. Appendix, the method of assessing psychosomatic risk (J. B. Stora).

Chapter One

1. cf. method in Appendix, particularly axis 1.

2. I will later present a case of masochistic pathology and somatic problems.
3. For a detailed description of the hypothalamic circuit, see Stora (2010b).

Chapter Two

1. Beyond my knowledge of neurosciences, I have greatly appreciated the works of Mark Solms in neuropsychoanalysis. I have carefully followed all his research, and I met him 15 years ago at the International Neuropsychoanalysis Association, of which he was president at the time.
2. In general, in the psychoanalytic societies of the International Psychoanalytical Association, the sessions are 45 minutes long; Freud often devoted an hour to his patients.
3. Here I am summarising some of the previous assessments of the symptoms.
4. The "mirror" function was developed by René Arpad Spitz (1965) and Jacques Lacan (1977).
5. It must be understood that the psychosomatician must proceed cautiously and carefully manage the quantum of emotional and mental excitations in each session, at risk of aggravating the somatic symptoms.

Chapter Three

1. Cf. psychosomatic nosography on the site: www.psychosomatique-integrative.net
2. The heart could no longer carry out the function of maintaining homeostasis; the patient was in great danger.

Chapter Four

1. The hereditary forms are rare (less than 5 per cent of cases), although a family medical history is discovered in nearly one fifth of cases.

Chapter Five

1. I discussed this at length in my work on organ transplants (Stora, 2005).
2. According to Grimaldi: "the chiropodical risk, that is the risk of amputation, is due to diabetic artertitis and neuropathy ... Gangrene of the extremities occurs 40 times more frequently in diabetics than in non-diabetics ... Neuropathy intervenes ... mainly by removing the painful perception; it removes the warning symptom that ensures the

protection of the feet against its many "enemies" … This gives rise to osteonecroses and painless fractures that cause nervous osteoarthropathy. These osteonecroses and fractures appear … in particular at the top of the foot's internal arch … Their fracture-necrosis-luxation causes the foot's internal arch to collapse. This is the classic diabetic Charcot's foot, with the formation of an enlarged flat foot that causes static problems that lead to calluses and neuropathic ulcerations." (Hartemann-Heurtier and Grimaldi *et al.*, 2009, pp. 232–234)
3. I am referring here to animal behaviour and the mammalian component of human beings.
4. See also Fleury (1997).

Chapter Six

1. An exam that used to be taken at the end of the first year of secondary school in France (*Brevet d'études du premier cycle*).
2. I should explain to readers who are not well informed about psychoanalytic psychosomatic interviews that the psychoanalyst often has to wait a very long time before he can understand all the information and all the patient's subjective experience in his relationship with himself, with the other and with specific others. Furthermore, patients need their complaints to be listened to and feel frustrated when they perceive emotional distance or a lack of empathy.
3. I should explain to the reader that I am reporting the patient's experience of her relationship with her doctor; I say "criticises" here rather than "the doctor points out", which is a more neutral expression.
4. This book (Le Quéré, 1998) was published long before my conversations with Gabrielle-Alicia. It tells the story of her marriage in detail, a story that did not occupy much of our conversations. At that time, Gabrielle had gained more serenity with regard to the dramatic events of her past. The interviews that I am reporting in this book are original and have not been developed in the above-mentioned text because they occurred after the organ transplant.
5. The patient is referring here to a fundamental problem relating to the interconnections between bodily changes and psychological adaptation to the body's new states.
6. A recent conversation with Alicia tells me about her current state; she is feeling better, although she is having to deal with many somatic problems caused by the treatment. She is having psychotherapy and making some progress. She is leading her life and helping her adolescent daughter to become an adult woman.

Chapter Seven

1. This is an observation of the "patient" Sigmund Freud, which is based on many documents, among others by Freud, Schur (1972), Jones (1972), and Anzieu (1986).
2. I would like to give my warmest thanks to my colleague Prof Daniel Thomas of the Institut de cardiologie at La Pitié-Salpêtrière for his permission to quote his written assessment in my book.

REFERENCES

Ancelin-Schützenberger, A. (1982). *Vocabulaire de base des sciences humaines* [Basic vocabulary of the human sciences]. Paris: Epi.
Anzieu, D. (1986). *Freud's Self-Analysis* (Trans. P. Graham). London: Hogarth.
Barnett, K., Mercer, S., Norbury, M., Watt, G., Wyke, S., & Guthrie, B. (2012). Epidemiology of multimorbidity and implications for health care, research, and medical education: a cross-sectional study. *Lancet*, pre-published online 10 May 2012 (doi:10.1016/S0140-6736(12)60240-2).
Bion, W. (1962). *Learning from Experience*. London: Tavistock.
Chen, P. (2010). Doctor and patient, losing touch with the patient. *The Annals of Family Medicine*.
Deutsch, F. (1949). *Applied Psychoanalysis: Selected Objectives of Psychotherapy*. New York: Grune and Stratton.
Deutsch, F. (1953). *The Psychosomatic Concept in Psychoanalysis*. New York: Int. Univ. Press.
Doidge, N. (2007). *The Brain that Changes Itself*. London: Penguin.
Dolto, F., & Séverin, G. (1982). *L'Évangile au risque de la psychanalyse*, Vol. 2 [1977]. Published in a shorter English edition as *Jesus of Psychoanalysis*. Garden City, NY: Doubleday, 1979.
Einstein, A. (1936). Physics and reality. In: *Out of My Later Years: The Scientist, Philosopher and Man Portrayed Through His Own Words*. London: Thames & Hudson, 1950.

Fleury, M. (1997). Nommer et classer les végétaux chez les Aluku (Boni) en Guyane française [Naming and classifying plants among the Aluku (Boni) in French Guiana]. *Actes du symposium "Indigenous Culture, Identity and Collective Rights in the Guyanas"*. Presented at the 49th International Congress of Americanists, Quito, 1997.

Fleury, M. (1999). Dénominations et représentations des végétaux en forêt tropicale: étude comparative chez les Amérindiens wayana et les Noirs marrons aluku de Guyane française [Names and representations of plants in the tropical forest: a comparative study among the Wayana Native Americans and the Aluku Maroon blacks of French Guiana]. Laboratoire d'Ethnobiologie-Biogéographie. Muséum National d'Histoire Naturelle, 57 rue Cuvier 75005 Paris, France.

Freud, S. (1916). *Introductory Lectures on Psycho-Analysis*. S.E., 15.

Gandjbakhch, I., Pavie, A., & Dorent, R. (2000). *Les journées de La Pitié 2000, insuffisance cardiaque et transplantation*. Paris: Novartis, R&J Éditions Médicales.

Giral, P., & Cuzin, E. (2004). *Le Cholestérol* [Cholesterol]. Paris: Belin.

Grace, W. J., & Graham, D. T. (1952). Relationship of specific attitudes and emotions to certain bodily diseases. *Psychosom. Med.*, *14*: 243–251.

Green, A. (2001). *Life Narcissism, Death Narcissism* (Trans. A. Weller). London: Free Association Books.

Grenand, P., & Grenand, F. (1996). Living in abundance. In: M. Ruiz-Perez & J. E. M. Arnold (Eds.), *Current Issues in Non-Timber Forest Products Research* (Chapter 10). CIFOR.

Hansel, B. (2007). *Surveillez votre ventre—Syndrome De La Bedaine*. [Watch your abdomen: metabolic syndrome]. Paris: Hachette.

Hartemann-Heurtier, A., Grimaldi, A., Halbron M., & Sachon C. (2009). *Guide pratique du diabète* [Practical guide to diabetes]. Paris: Masson.

Haynal, A., & Pasini, W. (1978/1984). *Médecine psychosomatique* [Psychosomatic Medicine] (second edition). Paris: Masson.

Jammer, M. (2011). *Einstein and Religion: Physics and Theology*. Princeton, NJ: Princeton University Press.

Jones, E. (1972). *Life and Work of Sigmund Freud*, Vol. 1. London, Hogarth.

Kubie, L. (1954). Psychiatric and psychoanalytic considerations of the problem of consciousness. In: J. F. Delafresnay (Ed.), *Brain Mechanisms and Consciousness, A Symposium*. Springfield, MA.

Kubie, L. (1961). Hypnotism. *Arch. Gen. Psychiat., IV*: 40–54.

Lacan, J. (1977). The mirror stage as formative of the function of the I. In: *Écrits: A Selection* (Trans. A. Sheridan). London: Routledge, pp. 1–8.

Lachowsky, M., & Winaver, D. (2011). *Aspects psychosomatiques de la consultation en gynécologie*. Paris: Elsevier Health Sciences.

Margolin, S. (1942). A physiological method for the induction of states of partial sleep, and securing free association and early memories in such states. *Trans. Amer. Neurol. Ass., 68*: 136–139.

Margolin, S., & Kubie, L. (1944a). An apparatus for the use of breath sounds as a hypnagogic stimulus. *American Journal of Psychiatry, 100*: 610.

Margolin, S., & Kubie, L. (1944b). The process of hypnotism and the nature of the hypnotic state. *American Journal of Psychiatry, 100*: 611–622.

Marty, P. (1976). *Les mouvements individuels de vie et de mort. Essai d'économie psychosomatique* [The individual movements of life and death: an essay on psychosomatic economy]. Vol. 1, Paris: Payot.

Marty, P., Herzberg, R., Stora, J. B. (1987). Organisation psychosomatique et risque de cancer [Psychosomatic organisation and cancer risk], research in December 1987, unpublished manuscript.

Marty, P., & Stora, J. B. (1988). La Classification psychosomatique Marty/ Ipso, méthode d'aide au diagnostic des organisations psychosomatiques et des maladies somatiques [the Marty/IPSO psychosomatic classification, a diagnostic tool for psychosomatic organisations and somatic illnesses]. *Médecine et Hygiène*.

Marty, P. (1990). *La psychosomatique de l'adulte* [Psychosomatics in Adults]. Paris: Presses Universitaires de France (Que sais-je? n° 1850).

Marty, P. (1994). *L'investigation Psychosomatique* [The Psychosomatic Investigation]. Paris: Presses Universitaires de France, Le Fil Rouge, pp. 47–74.

Marty, P., & Stora, J. B. (1989). *Psychosomatics*, ed. Beyrouth, in Arabic.

Masson, J. (1985). (Ed). *The Complete Letters of Sigmund Freud to Wilhelm Fliess 1887–1904*. Cambridge, MA and London: Belknap Press of Harvard University Press.

Nemiah, Sifneos, P. E. (1970). Affect and fantasy in patients with psychosomatic disorders. In: O. W. Hill (Ed.), *Modern Trends in Psychosomatic Medicine*. Boston: Butterworth, 1970.

Parat, C. (1994). L'affect partagé [Shared affect]. *Revue Française de psychanalyse, 6(25)*:

Pinel, P. (1798). *Nosographie philosophique, ou la méthode de l'analyse appliquée à la médecine*.

Purves, A., Fitzpatrick, K., La Mantia, A. -S., McNamara, J., & Williams, S. (Eds.) (2004). *Neurosciences*. Brussels: De Boeck.

Reich, W. (1927). Contribution in "Lay analysis". *International Journal of Psychoanalysis, 8*: 174–283.

Reich, W. (1972). *Character Analysis*. New York: Simon and Schuster.

Rosenberg, B. (1991). *Masochisme Mortifère et Masochisme Mardien de la Vie*. Paris: Presses Universitaires de France.

Roublev, A. (2012). La polypathologie devient la norme, à propos de médecine hyperspécialisée. [Multimorbidity is becoming the norm; on hyperspecialised medicine]. *Quotidien du Médecin*, 14/05/2012.

Saint-Exupéry, A. (1974). *The Little Prince* (Trans. K. Woods). London: Pan Books Ltd.

Salisbury, C. (2012). Multimorbidity: redesigning health care for people who use it. *Lancet*. Pre-published online 10 May 2012 (10.1016/S0140–6736(12)60482–6).

Schur, M. (1972). *Freud: Living and Dying*. New York, Int. Univ. Press.

Spitz, R. A. (1965). *The First Year of Life: A Psychoanalytic Study of Normal and Deviant Development of Object Relations*. New York: International Universities Press.

Stora, J. B. (1994). Sémiologie psychosomatique [Psychosomatic semiology]. *Annales de Psychiatrie, 9(2)*: 117–124.

Stora, J. B. (1995). Organisations mentales et maladies somatiques [mental organisations and somatic diseases]. *Annales de Psychiatrie, 10(1)*: 5–11.

Stora, J. B. (2005). *Vivre avec une Greffe, Accueillir l'autre* [Living with a Transplant, Receiving the other]. Paris: Odile Jacob.

Stora, J. B. (2007). *When the Body Displaces the Mind* (Trans. S. Leighton). London: Karnac.

Stora, J. B. (2010a). Le rôle de l'appareil psychique, des mécanismes neuronaux et neurohormonaux dans les somatisations: l'approche de la psychosomatique intégrative [the role of the psychic apparatus, neuronal and neurohormonal mechanisms in somatisations: the approach of integrative psychosomatics]. *Ann Med Psychol* (Paris) (2010), doi: 10.1016/j.amp.2009.09.018, available at: http://www.em-consulte.com/article/692422/article/le-role-de-lappareil-psychique-des-mecanismes-neur

Stora, J. B. (2010b). *Le Stress*. Paris: Presses Universitaires de France., collection "Que sais-je?" n° 2575; 1991; 8th edition, February 2010.

Stora, J. B. (2011). *La Neuropsychanalyse, Controverses et Dialogues* [Neuropsychoanalysis, Controversies and Dialogues]. Paris: MJW-Féditions.

Stora, J. B., Marty, P., & Gautier, J. -M. (1989). Sémiologie psychosomatique [Psychosomatic semiology]. *C.R n° 331: Groupe HEC*, Paris.

Uexküll, J. (1926). *Theoretical Biology*. London: Kegan Paul.

Uexküll, T. (1997). *Psychosomatic Medicine*. Philadelphia, PA: Lippincott, Williams and Wilkins.

Wolf, H. (1950). *Life Stress and Bodily Disease*. Baltimore, MD: Williams and Wilkins.

Zweig, S. (1933). *Mental Healers* (Trans. Eden & C. Paul). London: Cassell.

INDEX

abdominal obesity 9
adaptive reaction 116
adolescence 111
aggressive drives 6, 121
Ancelin-Schützenberge, A. xviii
anxiety 110
Anzieu, D. 124, 143
aphasic syndromes 22

Barnett, K. 81
Bemächtigungstrieb 65
"benevolent maternal role" 115
Bion, W. xxi, xxxix, 15, 36, 136
brain tumour patient, post-
surgery psychoanalysis/
psychotherapy of 21–47
  aphasic syndrome 22
  assessment of treatment after two years 42–46
  associations of ideas for 37–39

conflictual relationship with parents 25–26
continuation with anamnesis 26–28
dreams and 32–33
dynamic relationship and remembering 40–42
epileptic fits, diminishing 37–39
intersubjective intervention 40
meeting with neurosurgeon of 28–30
memory of words 21–26
mirror function, emergence of 33–35
motor cortices in 35–37
motricity of hand 35–37
necessary steps to improve condition of 31–32
neuronal and psychic deficiencies caused by operation 25

150 INDEX

neuronal problems experienced by 30–31
psychodynamic conflicts, emergence of 39–40
recall technique in 35–37

cardiac symptoms 124
"cardiac misery" 125
case studies
  Alicia 109–121
  Barbara 46–47
  Chloé 21–47
  Claude 49–60
  Damien 61–80
  Freud 124–128
  Lucien 85–107
  Marie-Laure 1–19
Chen, P. 140
"chronic myocarditis" 134
Cooper, C. 14
"combative spirit" 126
coronary thrombosis 131
countertransference 77
Cuzin, E. 9

Damasio, H. 23
Delattre, D. 29
Delattre, J. -Y. 29
Deutsch, F. xxi–xxii
Doidge, N. 28, 31, 46
Dolto, F. xvii
Dorent, R. 15
dual-control model 14

"ego ideal," 2
Einstein, A. xxxvi
Elderly heart patient, psychoanalysis/ psychotherapy of 49–60
  account of 53–54
  external object relationship 53
  history of 58–60

meeting with 51–53
overview 49–51
therapeutic process, continuation of 54–58
traumas, emergence of 58
eros activity 119
external object 4
external object relationship
  of elderly heart patient 53
  of metabolic syndrome patient 11–12

family discourse, and metabolic syndrome 3
Fitzpatrick, K. 24
Fleury, M. 106, 142
Freud, S. 3–5, 123, 126, 130–132, 137, 143

Gandjbakhch, I. 15
Giral, P. 9
grade II glioma 29
Green, A. 104–105
Grenand, F. 100
Grenand, P. 100
Grimaldi, A. 142
Guthrie, B. 81

Halbron, M. 142
Hansel, B. 9
Hartemann-Heurtier, A. 142
healing 123
Herzberg, R. 140
hypocholesterolaemic medication 118
hypochondriac patient, psychoanalysis/ psychotherapy 61–80
  cancer risk and remission in 65
  commentary 69–70
  conflict with women 70–80
  emotional suppression of 67

imaginary psychological
   dimension 62
MRI scan of 66
neurological examination of 64
problems of 61–67
psychic recovery 68–69
symptoms in 65–66
vertigo in 64–65
hypochondriac problem 134

influenza infection 134
Institute of Psychosomatics (IPSO)
   112–113, 138
integrative psychosomatics 81–83
Interpretation of Dreams 140
intersubjective intervention 40
intravenous drips 120

Jones, E. 143

kidney–pancreas transplant 110
komukomu (cucumber) 106
Kubie, L. xxii, 139

Lacan, J. 140–141
La Mantia, A. -S. 24
Lancet, The 83
Life Narcissism, Death Narcissism 105
limbic system 136
Little Prince, The 55–57, 137
L'officiel des spectacles 94

Margolin, S. xxii
Marty, P. 4, 14, 59, 140
"massed practice," 47
Masson, J. 125–129
maternal external object 3
medical disability 111
McNamara, J. 24
Mediterranean coast 118
Mental Healers 137
Mercer, S. 81

metabolic syndrome, psychoanalysis
   of female patient with 1–19
   abdominal obesity 9
   aggressive drives 6
   clinical interview 7–8
   consultation of medical file 8–9
   diagnostic criteria for 9
   "drive de-fusion," 3
   economic dimension in 3
   external object relationship 11–12
   family discourse and 3
   medical and psychosomatic
      predictions 12–14
   narcissism and 1
   object relationship 4, 13
   overview 1–7
   patient's isolation 7
   professional life and 5–6
   psychic functioning, assessment
      of 13
   psychosomatic clinical
      examination form 14–19
   psychosomatic risk 10–12
   psychosomatic risk assessment
      7–10
   relationship with parents 4–5
   stressful life and 1–2
"migraine attacks" 124
mirror function 33–35
motor cortices 35–37
"motoric insufficiency" 131
motricity of hand 35–37
multimorbidity 81–83
"mutative" interpretations 137

narcissistic wound 113
Nemiah, Sifneos, P. E. xxviii
"neuropathic ulceration," 105
Norbury, M. 81

obesity, abdominal 9
oligodendroglial tumours 29

pancreatitis 120
Paris School 134
paroxysmal tachycardia 130
Pavie, A. 15
physiotherapist 116
Pinel, P. xx
progressive disorganization 114
Prozac 67
pseudo-anginal pain 130
psychic
    domain 136
    equilibrium 117
    maturation process 115
    stress 126
psychoanalysis/psychotherapy
    following neurosurgery of brain
        tumour 21–47
    of elderly male with cardiac
        problem 49–60
    of female patient with metabolic
        syndrome 1–19
    of hypochondriac patient 61–80
    of type 2 diabetic patient
        85–107
psychoanalytic transference
    relationship 135
psychodynamic
    clinical examination form 14–19
    conflicts 39–40
    dimension 136
"psychosomatic" condition 131
psychosomatic conversation 5
psychosomatic interview 109
psychosomatic risk, in metabolic
    syndrome 10–12
    assessment 7–10
psychosomatic unity 118, 135
Purves, A. 24

Reich, W. xvi
Rosenberg, B. 53, 81–83
Roublev, A. 81–83

Sachon C. 142
Saint-Exupéry, A. 49, 52, 55, 57, 59–60
Salisbury, C. 81, 83
Schur, M. 124, 126–127, 130–132, 143
    comments 126
    description of the cardiac
        problems 126
    observations 131
Sévérin, G. xvii
skin allergies 117
somatic anxiety 54
somatic problems
    of hypochondriac patient 61–80
    of type 2 diabetic patient 88–90
somatic symptoms 119
spiritual path 117
Spitz, R. A. 118, 141
Stora, J. B. 14, 16, 19, 61, 69, 140
struggling diabetologists group 86
Studies on Hysteria 127–128
supportive psychotherapy 121
Surugue, P. 15

tachycardia and arrhythmia attacks
    131
therapeutic progression 135
transference neurosis 135
transference relationship 65
trauma, in elderly heart patient 58
traumatic marital experience 117
type 2 diabetic patient,
    psychoanalysis/
        psychotherapy of 85–107
    comprehensive learning
        approach based on
        observation for 99–100
    injury to narcissistic omnipotence
        87–88
    last meeting with psychotherapist
        102–104
    notes made by nurses 100–102
    overview 85–88

patient history 90–92
reflections and commentaries of
  104–107
role of culture of origin 92–94
somatic problems of 88–90
universe of Amazonian forest
  94–98
Wayampi world view 98–100

Uexküll, J. xxiii
Uexküll, T. xxv

vertigo 64–65

Watt, G. 81
Wayampi world view 98–100
When the Body Displaces the Mind
  61, 92
Williams, S. 24
Wolf, H. xxii
Wyke, S. 81

Zweig, S. 137–138